Heythrop College

1614-2014

A Commemorative History

Michael J Walsh

Heythrop College

University of London

2014

Published by

Heythrop College
University of London
Kensington Square
London W8 5HN

Telephone: 020 7795 6600
Fax: 020 7795 4200

www.heythrop.ac.uk

ISBN: 978-0-9929168-0-0

Printed by Westprint, Exeter

CONTENTS

LIST OF ILLUSTRATIONS

THE COLLEGE COAT OF ARMS

The arms of the College were formally granted to the College by Royal Licence on 10th September 1973. By chance one member of the Library staff at the time had worked at the College of Heralds and was a considerable help in the design.

The original intention had been to include two Talbot dogs as "supporters", to recall the Shrewsbury (family name Talbot) connection both with the English, later British, Province of the Society of Jesus and more directly with Heythrop Hall in Oxfordshire (see below).

In the centre of the escutcheon is the Golden Lion of Brabant, recalling the College's link with Louvain and Liège, while the silver and blue lozenges acknowledge the patronage of the Wittelsbach family, the Archdukes of Bavaria: they appear on the flag of Bavaria. The cross and the nails of the Passion are the traditional symbol, and the seal, of the Society of Jesus from the time of its Founder, St Ignatius Loyola.

Heythrop College, Oxfordshire, 1926 - 1970

ACKNOWLEDGEMENTS

A good many people have helped me, one way or another, in the preparation of this account of Heythrop's four hundred years existence.

I am particularly grateful to the current Principal, Fr Michael Holman SJ, who commissioned the work, or at least encouraged me to think about engaging upon it, when he was still Provincial of the British Province. Immediately before coming to the College, however, he took a few months sabbatical leave and it was during the period of his absence that a firm decision to go ahead was made by the Acting Principal, Fr James Sweeney CP. The Library staff at Heythrop were unfailingly helpful, arranging for books to be brought in for me from off-site storage, so my thanks to the librarians and especially to Vicky Rowley. Annabel Clarkson, now in charge of External Relations in the Principal's office, found for me the (admittedly large and sturdy) cardboard box which contains the files relating to the move to Cavendish Square. When the footnotes cite "Heythrop Archives" it is to this box that I am referring!

In the course of writing this short book I visited the considerably more complex Jesuit archives in Rome, the Maryland Province archives at Georgetown University in Washington DC, the Copleston papers at Boston College in Boston Massachusetts, and the Jesuit archive in London. I should like to express my appreciation of the immense help I received from the staff of all these collections, especially from Anna Edwards in London.

Many individuals have also assisted me greatly. I would particularly like to thank Fr John (always known as Jack) Mahoney SJ for his comments on the chapter concerned with Heythrop in Cavendish Square and Professor Maurice Whitehead of Swansea University who has worked on the Jesuit school at St Omer, Bruges and Liège: his subsequent volume is referred to in the pages which follow. He sent me reams of material that he had collected in Liège, all of which was immensely useful and saved me from (some) errors. He also very kindly read the text and saved me from a great deal of time and trouble. Fr Tom McCoog SJ knows far more about at least some of this story than I do and he was a great help when starting out. His unpublished thesis for the University of Warwick on the finances of the early English Jesuits was indispensable. Fr Michael Barnes SJ reminded me of some details of the last years of Heythrop in Oxfordshire, and of the early years in London. Bro James Hodkinson SJ was very helpful in providing photographs from the Jesuit provincial archives. I am most grateful to all those who commented on the draft.

Finally I ought to mention that the publication *Letters and Notices*, from which I have often quoted, is not strictly speaking in the public domain: it is the "house organ" of the British Province and is intended "ad usum tantum nostrum", as it says on its cover, "for the use of Ours only", meaning it is for Jesuit eyes alone. I am most grateful, therefore, for permission to quote from articles published in it by the late Fr Bruno Brinkman SJ, and by Jesuit Fathers Brendan Callaghan, Michael Kirwan and Jack Mahoney. Without these articles, and especially the long two-part piece by Fr Mahoney, compiling the history of the College since 1970 would have been difficult, if not impossible. The title *Letters and Notices* is abbreviated to its customary LLNN. The other abbreviation in the footnotes, ABSI, is for the Archives of the British Province of the Society of Jesus.

Michael J Walsh
30th March 2014

FOREWORD

In this academic year 2013-2014, Heythrop College is celebrating the 400th anniversary of its foundation as a college for the study of theology and philosophy by the English Jesuits in Louvain in 1614. Michael Walsh has written this History of the College to commemorate this remarkable achievement.

Most readers of this History will, like me, only be familiar with Heythrop as a constituent college of the University of London. Located firstly in Cavendish Square and since 1993 in Kensington Square, the College has grown significantly to number more than 800 undergraduate, postgraduate and research students coming from Britain and more than twenty countries overseas. Very small in university terms the College may be, it is nonetheless one of the largest centres for our two specialist subjects in the country.

Those of us associated with the College today recognise that we owe a great debt of gratitude to those who in the 1970s established Heythrop as a college of the University. In the years immediately after the Second Vatican Council, the Church was encouraging lay men and women to participate in ministry and one of the hopes the Society of Jesus had for the new Heythrop was that it should make a significant contribution to educating a theologically and philosophically literate laity. Undergraduate and postgraduate programmes, full-time and part-time, taught during the day and in the evenings, were developed to further this mission. Heythrop's students have gone on to make significant contributions to the life of the Church, in the academic world, in education and the parish and in wider Church life and few could doubt that this hope has been substantially realised.

It was also hoped that Heythrop College located in London would provide a more suitable setting for the education of future priests and ministers of the Church, one which would prepare them better to preach the Gospel to the people of their day. The city afforded a greater variety of opportunities for pastoral experience and training while the University offered a more rigorous intellectual formation alongside some of those very people to whom these students would later minister. In 2007, Heythrop was designated the English-speaking centre in Europe for Jesuit priestly formation and Jesuit scholastics are today joined in their studies by diocesan seminarians and students from other religious orders and congregations. Indeed, the College's significance as a place for such training was further underlined in January of this year by the revival of the ecclesiastical faculties of philosophy and theology, together known as the Bellarmine Institute.

My predecessors as Principal - two of whom, Brendan Callaghan and John McDade, led the College for more than half of its existence in London - ensured that Heythrop also played its part in the intellectual life of the Church, the University and wider society. *The Heythrop Journal* has maintained its place as one of the leading scholarly publications in theology and philosophy and our more recently established institutes and centres explore the interface of religion and society, Christianity and other religions, faith and secularism. Meanwhile for many of our students, coming as they now do from many faith traditions and from none, their years at Heythrop have provided them with a unique opportunity to explore theological and philosophical questions in the context of a scholarly community with a long Catholic tradition. In these ways, the College has become one of the principal means whereby the Jesuits in Britain contribute to the mission given to the whole Society by Pope Benedict XVI and his predecessors to work on the frontiers where faith and modern culture meet.

Those who have only known the College in London will want to join me in thanking Michael Walsh for accepting the challenge to write in the space of little more than 50,000 words a history not only of this generation but of the great many that went before. Michael provides us with a particular kind of history, an institutional history illustrated with a wealth of significant detail. The fact that Heythrop has been in continuous existence longer than any other theology college in the Society of Jesus is due to the capacity it has displayed time and again to accommodate itself to changing religious, political and educational circumstances. Michael explains what it has meant for - and sometimes cost - the College and those involved with it to adapt in this way. In the pages that follow, we encounter many of the problems, often very challenging ones, the changes of policy, the people and of course the personalities involved in the various transformations which the College has undergone both in its more recent and its more distant past.

If adaptation was important in years gone by, we can be sure it will be no less important in the future. We can only marvel at the hard work and determination of the many who, in the course of our four centuries, have laboured to ensure that the College maintained and developed its mission in the midst of so many changes - as we trust, with God's help, in God's way, it will continue to do for a long time to come.

Michael Holman SJ
Principal
30th April 2014

PREFACE

When Heythrop College opened its doors in the autumn of 1970 as part of London University the person presiding over it as the College's new - strictly speaking its first - Principal[1] was Fr Frederick Copleston. He had been appointed to the post not because of his administrative ability but because, as he disarmingly remarks in his Memoirs,[2] "within a limited academic field my name was known as a writer on philosophical topics". As author of the nine volumes of what is probably the best-known and most widely-admired history of philosophy in the English language, his own description of himself is something of an understatement, but, as he implies, being a historian of philosophy did not particularly prepare him for the task of running a new College. For, as he also remarks,[3] it was indeed "technically" a new College although "there was obviously a real element of continuity".

As Heythrop is celebrating its fourth centenary the question of continuity is a very real one. Can Heythrop College, University of London, claim direct descent from the house of studics founded in Louvain in 1614 for the education of Jesuit priests? If it can, it is the oldest institution in the Society of Jesus with a continuous history, surviving as an entity even the papal suppression of the Society between 1773 and 1814. Those dates do not give the whole picture for, as will be seen, the English Jesuits had re-established their province, that is to say their administrative region, a dozen years before the formal restoration by Pope Pius VII.

It is true that the College has existed in several different locations. It was first in Louvain then, for the longest single period of time (1624-1794), in Liège in what is now, but was not then, Belgium. Next it was at Stonyhurst in Lancashire followed, for the theologians, by nearly a century at St Beuno's not far from St Asaph in North Wales. From 1926 to 1970 the College was situated at Heythrop Hall in Oxfordshire, hence the name, and even during its relatively short time in London as part of the University it has occupied two sites, one at Cavendish Square in central London, the other - and present -

1 This may seem a rather obvious title for the head of a college, but as far as Heythrop was concerned it was a complete innovation. Traditionally Jesuit colleges had (and many still have) rectors, who governed the community, and prefects of studies who oversaw the teaching.

2 Frederick C. Copleston, *Memoirs of a Philosopher* (Kansas City, MO, Sheed and Ward, 1993), p.165.

3 Copleston, *Memoirs*, p.164.

one in Kensington Square. Quite apart from the suppression of the Society, therefore, it might seem to be something of a challenge to demonstrate continuity over the centuries.

There is of course a clear link in the association with the Society of Jesus, but there is much more than that. As Copleston remarked in the passage just cited, students moved from one location to another, and so did staff and library. That is true not only of the relocation from Oxfordshire to London, but at every change in the four hundred-year history. Even when the Society of Jesus was suppressed staff and students for the most part remained in place. And then, a couple of decades later, the community and its pupils moved across the Channel en masse with at least some of its books to the secure remoteness of Stonyhurst.

Moreover, there was another element of continuity which is not so often remarked upon. Jesuits of the English province worked also in colonial Maryland. After the suppression, the now former Jesuit John Carroll, who had been born in Maryland, returned there from Liège and in time became the superior of the mission, and later the first Bishop of Baltimore. To provide for Catholic education in the region under his charge he founded an academy at Georgetown which eventually became Washington DC's Georgetown University. As Professor Maurice Whitehead has remarked, some of the former students of the Academy in Liège joined the staff of the new academy, and although none of the pupils are known to have migrated from Europe to America, some of the families who had sent their elder sons to Liège, now sent their younger ones to Bishop Carroll's foundation.[1] Like Heythrop, therefore, Georgetown University has links, albeit remotely, with that first foundation at Louvain.

1 "A prolific nursery of piety and learning", in Thomas McCoog (ed.), *Promising Hope* (Rome: Institutum Historicum Societatis Iesu, 2003), pp.144-145.

LOUVAIN, 1614

The Society of Jesus, the Jesuits, is commonly thought of as a religious order in the Catholic Church dedicated to teaching, whether in schools or in universities. Although they do many other things as well - they are, for instance, astronomers,[1] spiritual directors, missionaries - that is a fair description. It was the first religious order to make education a major part of their *raison d'être* - or "charism", as those who write about the spiritual lives of members of religious orders and congregations might want to put it. It was, however, a mission far from the minds of the followers of Iñigo de Loyola (he changed his name to Ignatius under the misapprehension that it was a Latinised version of Iñigo) when they first took their vows in a chapel on Montmartre in Paris on 15th August 1534. Apart from committing themselves in these vows to a life of poverty - as priests, they were already committed to chastity - they each undertook to make a pilgrimage to Jerusalem (Ignatius had already been, the others in the end never went) and then to offer themselves to the pope of the day to work in whatever capacity he thought fit. Consequently they all came together again in Rome. There in 1540 Pope Paul III formally created the Society of Jesus with the bull *Regimini militantis ecclesiae*. The bull incorporated what was called "The Formula of the Institute", a very brief statement drawn up by Ignatius of how, within the Society, the members should live their lives.

The very first Jesuits were all graduates of the University of Paris. It was therefore natural that some of them should be immediately put to work lecturing in theology - in Rome, in Mainz, in Ingolstadt. A papal bull of 1547 gave them permission to teach anywhere - an exceptional privilege - and to teach anything. The Formula of the Institute had envisaged colleges run by the Society, but despite the name these were not to be teaching institutions. They were more like residences than colleges in the modern sense of the word, where student Jesuits - scholastics as they were called - would live while attending classes at nearby universities. The earliest batch of scholastics were sent to just such a college attached to the University of Paris, but in 1542 the outbreak of war between France and the Holy Roman Empire meant that subjects of the Empire had to leave Paris. They went instead to Louvain.

---

1 Jesuits staff the two Vatican observatories, at Castel Gandolfo, the papal summer residence near Rome, and at Tucson in Arizona.

By 1544 there were seven of these "colleges", at the universities of Paris, Louvain, Cologne, Padua, Alcalá, Valencia and Coimbra in Portugal. Unlike other houses of the Society, the colleges were to be endowed: Ignatius did not want the students to be concerned, as he himself had been, with the burden of raising money, it was more important that they should get on with their studies. There was some teaching, above all in a large college in Goa, but at the start that was the exception. However, the situation changed remarkably quickly. The catalyst was Francisco de Borja,[1] the Duke of Gandia, a future superior general of the order and, incidentally, a canonised saint. After founding a college attached to the University of Valencia he decided he should have one in Gandia itself. Gandia did not have a university. In Gandia's newly-founded Jesuit college, therefore, Jesuit scholastics were students while Jesuit professors did the teaching. It was not only Jesuits who attended the classes, however, but laymen as well. This model inspired the Viceroy of Sicily to petition for a similar college in Messina, to be funded by the authorities of the city. This was a major departure, for though scholastics would study - and teach - at Messina, its primary purpose was to serve the young men of the city who could there study every discipline up to what we would now call tertiary level, everything, that is, except law and medicine. Other colleges swiftly followed along the same lines. In February 1551 the Roman College, renamed the Gregorian University in 1584 after its patron Pope Gregory XIII, started taking students. "Over its door hung the inscription 'School of Grammar, Humanities, and Christian Doctrine', Free".[2]

"The Jesuits' ideals were socially conservative", writes John W. O'Malley. "It never occurred to them that they should make concerted efforts to break down traditional roles and class structures ... they depended for the endowment of their schools on the wealthy and powerful. They opened their

1 In Italian Borgia, a name by which he is more frequently known. He was the great grandson of Rodrigo Borgia, the ill-famed Pope Alexander VI.

2 John W. O'Malley, *The First Jesuits* (Cambridge MA, Harvard University Press, 1993), p. 205. Much of the preceding section has been drawn from Fr O'Malley's excellent book, especially pp. 32 and 200-205. For the Gregorian, see Philip Caraman, *The University of the Nations* (New York, Paulist Press, 1981).

schools, however, to all who were qualified and who would abide by their rules".[1] The colleges served rich and poor alike, although the curriculum, with its emphasis on the humanities, was more likely to appeal to the former rather than the latter. While the colleges might have been open to all, without charge, they had originally been established for the education of scholastics and that remained the case. What made this strikingly different from the seminary training of diocesan priests was that scholastics studied philosophy and theology not in closed groups of their own kind, but alongside lay people even when they were doing so in Jesuit-run institutions.[2]

Messina, then, was the prototype college, but it was more than that. Just about the time that the Roman College was opened a document was produced entitled *De ratione studiorum Messanae*, or "On the system of study at Messina", perhaps as a way of spreading best practice. This statement of how things were done in Sicily was the forerunner of a set of instructions for all Jesuits, superiors and schoolmasters alike, formally known as *Ratio atque Institutio Studiorum Societatis Iesu* though usually simply called the *Ratio Studiorum*, which was printed at Naples in 1598 but only issued the following year.[3] It opens with the words "It is the principal ministry of the Society of Jesus to educate youth in every branch of knowledge that is in keeping with its Institute. The aim of our educational program is to lead men to the knowledge and love of our Creator and Redeemer".[4] It was the implementation of the *Ratio* which made Jesuits the leading educationalists in the seventeenth century.

It had many different sections, but fundamentally it laid down what was to be taught in Jesuit colleges. The first members of the Society were men of the Renaissance, not of the Middle Ages. Their formation at the

1 O'Malley, *First Jesuits*, p. 211.

2 The comparison is, it has to be admitted, a little anachronistic because seminaries, theological colleges in each diocese, were only mandated by a 1563 decree of the Council of Trent and then took a considerable time to develop Church-wide.

3 An interim version had been published in 1591.

4 The 1970 translation by Allan P. Farrell is available online at http://admin.wyk.edu.hk/documents/A01%20Jesuit%20Education%20&%20Ignatian%20Pedagogy/Ratio%20Studiorum.htm, accessed 21 February 2013.

University of Paris had been in the humanist tradition. Even in the Society's Constitution, officially approved in 1558, the study of Aristotle was required as the foundation of the philosophical disciplines, and this was quoted in the *Ratio*, though with the proviso that if the teachings of Aristotle contradicted the Faith they were to be refuted. Similarly, the *Ratio* laid down that the theologian to be studied was Thomas Aquinas, though even in the case of Aquinas a degree of distance from his teachings might be allowed, provided, it would seem, that the Jesuit interpreters of St Thomas did not go out of their way to be different from absolutely everybody else. There was a degree of openness written into the instructions to Jesuit lecturers, both in philosophy and theology.[1] As will be seen later, this attitude was not without its problems when it came to scientific research. In 1633 Galileo was condemned by the Roman Inquisition for teaching a heliocentric cosmology because it appeared to contradict the faith. But in his *Almagestum Novum* of 1651 Giovanni Battista Riccioli SJ wrote of the condemnation " as there has been no definition on this matter by the Sovereign Pontiff or by a General Council directed and approved by him, it is in no way of faith that the sun moves and the earth is motionless; ... Still, all Catholics are obliged ... at least not to firmly teach the opposite of what the decree lays down".[2] There was a copy of the *Almagestum* in the library of the College at Liège which may have helped, for, as Louis Caruana has commented,[3] Jesuits were obliged to "trace a risky path across slippery intellectual territory". As will be seen, this controversy was to impinge upon the staff of the English College, but in 1614, just as the Roman Inquisition started to interest itself in Galileo's

---

1 "In this intellectual freedom", wrote John Henry Newman of the Jesuits in the second volume of his *Historical Sketches*, "its members justly glory; inasmuch as they have set their affections, not on the opinions of the Schools, but on the souls of men. And it is the same charitable motive which makes them give up the poetry of life, the poetry of ceremonies - of the cowl, the cloister, and the choir - content with the most prosaic architecture, if it be but convenient, and the most prosaic neighbourhood, if it be but populous" (London, Longmans Green & Co., 1899), pp. 369-70.

2 Quoted by Louis Caruana in his article "The Jesuits and the Scientific Revolution" in Thomas Worcester (ed.), *The Cambridge Companion to the Jesuits* (Cambridge University Press, 2008), p. 247, italics added. This paragraph draws heavily on Caruana's article, pp. 245-247.

3 Caruana, Jesuits, p. 210.

writings, the future Heythrop was opening its doors in Louvain.

In the history of the English Jesuits, Doña Luisa de Carvajal y Mendoza deserves more attention than she is customarily given.[1] She was a wealthy orphan, brought up by uncles and aunts, but as soon as she could live independently she adopted the life of a nun in her own house in Madrid, though without joining a religious order. Inspired by the martyrdom in York of the Jesuit Henry Walpole in 1595, she decided herself to seek martyrdom and travelled to England in 1605, arriving in London penniless just after the persecution of Catholics that followed the Gunpowder Plot. The Jesuit superior, Henry Garnet, managed to dissuade her from her desire to die for the faith, but she was, nonetheless, twice imprisoned and died in 1614 aged 52 in the house of the Spanish ambassador shortly after being released from gaol. Her remains were taken back to Spain the following year, and she was buried in Madrid's Royal Convent of the Incarnation.[2]

But that is not where she had wanted to be interred. In her will, drawn up in Valladolid just before her journey to London, she asked that "some little place" be found for her body in a church of the Society[3] and donated a considerable sum of money to open a noviceship for those Englishmen seeking to join the Jesuits.[4] At the time there was no province - no regional government of the Order - for England: a vice province was created only in 1619, and a full province in January 1623. But there were plenty of men offering themselves to the Society, and a place was needed, a

1 See *This Tight Embrace: Luisa de Carvajal y Mendoza* (1566-1614), edited, translated and introduced by Elizabeth Rhodes (Milwaukee, Marquette University Press, 2000) and Glyn Redworth, *The She-Apostle: The Extraordinary Life and Death of Luisa de Carvajal* (Oxford University Press, 2008).

2 "There were Catholics who were executed for lesser crimes against the English state than Carvajal committed single-handedly: she went so far as to establish a feminine version of the Society in downtown London" Elizabeth Rhodes, "Join the Jesuits, See the World: Early Modern Women" in John W. O'Malley et al., (eds.), *The Jesuits II: Cultures, Sciences and the Arts, 1540-1773* (Toronto, University of Toronto Press, 2006), p. 45.

3 Francis Edwards, *The Jesuits in England* (Tunbridge Wells, Burns and Oates, 1985), p. 49

4 There is a slight disagreement about how much the donation was. Edwards says 1,400 ducats and Thomas McCoog, in his unpublished thesis, *The Society of Jesus in England 1623-1688: An Institutional Study* (doctoral dissertation, Warwick University, May 1984), says 1,200.

noviceship, where they could receive the standard Jesuit formation and where their vocations might be tested. Hitherto they had been dependent on the good will of the Belgian province[1] to provide for potential recruits, but the Belgian provincial limited entry into his noviceship by Englishmen to only two a year.

There was a suggestion that Luisa de Carvajal's money should be spent in buying a property in Bilbao in Northern Spain, but this was opposed by Robert Persons, perhaps the most influential English Jesuit of the day, on the grounds that it was too far from England, and that the climate was unsuitable for Englishmen.[2] There were already a number of English institutions created by and for men and women who had been forced to flee England because of their faith[3] in the Spanish Netherlands, including a successful school started by the Jesuits at St Omer[4]. In the end it appears to have been the Jesuit General in Rome, Claudio Acquaviva, who decided the matter, suggesting that Louvain might be an appropriate location. Persons therefore bought a property - it had formerly belonged to the Knights of Malta and was consequently known as St John's - which stood on high ground just within the city walls. It was to house not just the novices but also older men in retirement from the rigours of the English mission. Of the first novices who entered the Society when the noviceship opened on 1st February 1607, six of the entrants were already priests, two who were scholastics, and five who wished to be lay-brothers.[5]

The choice of Louvain was significant. There was already a Jesuit

---

1 The Belgian province was created in 1564. In 1612, having grown extremely large, it was split in two along linguistic lines. Louvain fell into the Flemish-speaking "Flandro-Belge" province, while the other houses - the school at St Omer, the establishments at Watten and Liège - lay within the "Gallo-Belge", or French-speaking (Walloon), province.

2 Hubert Chadwick, *St Omers to Stonyhurst* (London, Burns and Oates, 1962), p. 50.

3 They were known as recusants, because they refused (*recuso* is the Latin for "I refuse") to attend Church of England services or take the oath of allegiance.

4 Chadwick, *St Omers*, p. 38: "In eight years St Omers had outstripped in numbers the English college of Douay or indeed any of the English or Scottish seminaries on the continent". St Omers College had originally been called a seminary.

5 Edwards, *The Jesuits*, p. 49.

college there attached to the ancient university and Jesuits, most particularly the controversial theologian Leonard Lessius, who had retired from teaching in 1601 but remained in the college and continued to write, were among its professors.[1] It is not surprising, therefore, that before long English Jesuit students were sent to live in the noviceship while attending lectures in the university. Jesuit regulations required that novices be kept apart from scholastics, so in 1614 a new house was built for the former in St Johns's substantial garden, leaving the Louvain house to the scholastics. It was this modest event, the move of the novices into their new building - though their stay in it was short - and the handing over of the original noviceship to the training of scholastics that marked the start of the English Jesuit theological college.[2]

The novices, as has been seen, were well provided for by Doña Luisa's gift. Funding the scholastics who stayed behind at Louvain when, by the end of 1615 the novices had all moved to Liège,[3] was rather more of a problem. Jesuits, with their vow of poverty, were expected to live on alms, to sustain themselves by begging, in other words. That is what Ignatius Loyola had done throughout his student years, once even travelling to London, financially a particularly successful trip he afterwards recorded. He was not, however, in favour of the Society's students begging, on the grounds that it got in the way of their studies. He therefore laid it down that houses where there were Jesuits in training were to be provided with adequate funds for their upkeep so that students would not be be distracted from their learning by the need to seek alms. The situation of the English scholastics was eased by a gift from Thomas Sackville, son of the first Earl of Dorset, who donated

1 The future Jesuit saint, Robert Bellarmine, went there first as a student in 1569 and remained there as a professor until 1576.

2 Edwards, *The Jesuits*, "In 1614 St John's ... sprouted a college of philosophy and theology".

3 It is possible that Liège had always been the intended site of the novitiate. In Volume I, "Works in Languages other than English" of their *The Contemporary Printed Literature of the English Counter- Reformation between 1558 and 1640* (Aldershot, Scolar Press, 1989) the late David Rogers and Anthony Allison list a document by the Prince Bishop of Liège, Ernest of Bavaria, addressed to the clergy of his diocese and "appealing for alms to help establish the English Jesuit novitiate". The appeal, no. 738 in their bibliography, is undated, but must be before the death of Ernest in 1612.

£200 immediately and established a fund for the future of 40,000 ducats.[1] Around the same time an unnamed benefactor (McCoog speculates that it was once again Thomas Sackville[2]) said he wanted to found a college to train priests to do battle against heresy. Acquaviva accepted the donation on 13th October 1612.

So the founding of the college of philosophy and theology was a modest affair, the gift of a considerable sum in 1612 to provide for the upkeep of student priests, and the move of the novices from St John's, Louvain, to a new house in Liège. But Liège was to prove only a temporary location for the novices. The Bishop of St Omer, a Franciscan, who was a good friend of the (Belgian) rector of the school, proposed to hand over to the Society a former monastery of canons located at Watten, a village some seven miles north of St Omer. Negotiations dragged on for four years or so, even the Spanish King taking an interest, until in 1608 Pope Paul V issued a bull, dissolving the canonry. The intention was that the English Jesuits should then take it over, but this did not happen, probably because of the opposition of Sir Thomas Lowndes, the English ambassador from 1604 until 1609 at the court of the governor of the Spanish Netherlands, the Archduke Albert.[3] Lowndes was very close to the Archduke and Isabella the Archduchess, naming his daughter Isabella, and the Archduchess became her godmother. The ambassador had also tried to prevent Persons buying St John's in 1606, but obviously without success.

The property at Watten had finally come into the Society's possession in 1611 but was used by the Belgian Jesuits rather than English ones. Though

---

1 McCoog, *The Society of Jesus*, p. 78. Thomas's father, the first Earl of Dorset (1536-1608), who was also named Thomas, had held high office under both Elizabeth and James I, and had become extremely wealthy. Though the elder Thomas was a Protestant, his mother had been a devout Catholic and he was as tolerant as his position allowed him to be of the religious convictions of his neighbours and of those within his own family.

2 McCoog, *The Society of Jesus*, p. 79.

3 Mark Greengrass, 'Edmondes, Sir Thomas (d. 1639)', *Oxford Dictionary of National Biography*, Oxford University Press, 2004); online edn, Jan 2008 [http://www.oxforddnb.com/view/article/8486, accessed 24 April 2013]. Lowndes then became ambassador in Paris (1610-17).

Lowndes was no longer on the scene, he had been replaced by his protégé William Trumbull, who was, if anything, even more staunchly Protestant, and antipathetic to the Jesuits, than his predecessor. It was not until 1623 that the English novices finally moved into their new home at Watten. By this time the Archduke was dead and Isabella was sole governor. It was not so much that she was more sympathetic to the English Jesuits but the political situation had changed. There was much talk of a Spanish marriage for King Charles I, and with relations between England and Spain rapidly improving, she had less to fear from the machinations of the ambassador. With the novices ensconced at Watten there was now a property available at Liège, and there the scholastics, the students of philosophy and theology, moved in 1624 from St John's in Louvain.

LIEGE 1624

From the tenth century the strategic city of Liège had been a Prince-Bishopric; the Prince-Bishop, at least in the 17th and 18th centuries when they came from the Wittelsbach family of Bavaria, was an Elector of the Holy Roman Empire by virtue of being also the Archbishop of Cologne. It was at some distance from the Channel ports and therefore, as far as the English Jesuits were concerned, mercifully freer than Louvain, and even more so than St Omer, from the attention of English spies. That may indeed have been one of its attractions as a location for the noviceship, and perhaps even more so as a house of studies where the scholastics were much freer to enter the town than the novices had been.

It also already had close links to the Society.[1] In 1561 Pope Pius IV had issued a bull for the establishment of what was called a "collegium publicum" to be run by the Jesuits for the education of the diocesan clergy, as required by the decrees of the Council of Trent. But it is clear that the Prince-Bishop of the day had greater ambitions, and was thinking of opening what would in effect be a university. The plan foundered because of the hostility of the University of Louvain which claimed that Pope Martin V's bull of its foundation in 1425 granted it a monopoly in what we would now call tertiary education. The plan for the seminary was therefore dropped and in 1582 the Belgian Jesuits opened a college instead.

This was under a new Prince-Bishop, Ernest of Bavaria, who at the Roman College had been an outstanding pupil of the brilliant Jesuit mathematician Christopher Clavius. He fulfilled the requirements of Trent by setting up both a minor seminary at Saint-Trond, then part of the principality of Liège, in 1589 and a major seminary in Liège itself in 1592. A few years later the major seminary was entrusted to the Jesuits, who promptly expanded the curriculum to include dialectics, at which the University of Louvain again protested and, under threat of excommunication, they had to abandon the plan.

1 Much of what follows in the next two paragraphs depends on Camélia Opsomer, "Un foyer d'études sous l'Ancien Régime : le Collège des Jésuites anglais de Liège", *Bulletin de l'Académie royale de Belgique*, 6e série, t. XII, 1-6 (2001), pp. 11-39, but available on the University of Liège's website, http://www.gedhs.ulg.ac.be/ebibliotheque/articles/opsomer/college.html#asterisque, accessed 26 April 2013.

The Bishop therefore opened a residence in Louvain to provide an opportunity for his brighter candidates for the priesthood to pursue the study of theology to a higher level. The Walloon Jesuits did not give up hope. In 1613 the Rector of their College made another attempt, but again the University protested, and was backed up by Archduke Albert. In 1624, after the death of Albert, the Rector of the Liège College made yet another attempt, but this time he encountered the opposition not only of the University of Louvain but also that of one of the longest-serving Jesuit Generals,[1] Mutius Vitelleschi (1615-45).

These attempts by the Walloon Jesuits to establish a university happened either before the English novices arrived, or just after they had left for Watten, but their superiors would undoubtedly have been aware of them. Liège, therefore, appeared an attractive place to set up the English college, far enough away from the Channel coast, with a feisty Walloon community already in residence, and a Prince-Bishop who was extremely supportive of the Society of Jesus.

The friendship of the Prince-Bishop proved to be particularly important. The Liège property had been acquired in 1613 by John Gerard for the novices at a cost of 1000 florins and a rent of 150 florins. The money was provided by William Browne, a lay brother[2], the soldier Sir William Stanley who had famously (or infamously) abandoned the service of Elizabeth for that of Spain, and Sir George Talbot, later Earl of Shrewsbury, both Stanley and Talbot being cousins of Fr Gerard.[3] It has been suggested[4] that it may have been Talbot who persuaded Archduke Maximilian I of Bavaria to provide funds

1 Until the retirement of Pedro Arrupe in September 1983 after suffering a stroke, Jesuit Superior Generals had served for life. He had in fact suffered the stroke in August 1981, but instead of allowing him to call a General Congregation to elect a successor, Pope John Paul II appointed an interim Vicar General, not the one of Arrupe's own choosing.

2 "Though grandson, brother and uncle of a Viscount (his grandfather was Queen Mary's ambassador to the Holy See) [he] was content to spend his life in the humble duties of a Jesuit Lay-Brother", Henry Foley, *Records of the English Province of the Society of Jesus*, vol. V (London, Burns and Oates, 1879), p. 186.

3 Foley, *Records*, p. 186.

4 By Geoffrey Holt for instance, cf. 'The English Jesuits at Liège and Chevremont' in *Chevremont Un tricentaire, Un millenaire*, 1988, p. 111.

for the College. But that seems an unnecessary supposition. The Prince-Bishop at the time of the purchase was Ferdinand of Bavaria[1] and when the scholastics moved in thirteen years later he was still there. He had been educated by the Jesuits at Ingolstadt and as bishop worked conscientiously to implement the reforming decrees of the Council of Trent despite the fact that his own multiplicity of benefices was flatly contrary to the intentions of the Council. He was close to his older brother Archduke Maximilian, who had also received a Jesuit education, which may be why Maximilian and his pious first wife Elizabeth of Lorraine decided to endow the fledgling college. They gave 6,000 scudi, with an annual return of 2,813 scudi, to be paid in perpetuity. The donation was accepted by Vitelleschi on 20th May 1627.

Rumours spread rapidly as to the size of the gift, [2] and the General advised the Provincial that he ought to let people know just how large it was because the Rector of the College was alarmed lest exaggerated reports should put off other potential donors. The new endowment allowed the college to support 15 extra people but the community living in the College frequently rose above an economic number and the treasurer often had difficulty balancing his budget, in which case the community had to depend on alms, and to ensure it collected any money owing to it. There were of course other sources of income. There were properties on the continent and in England - including two vineyards near Rome - which produced rents. The complications of the college taking over the building intended originally for the noviceship meant that the finances of both institutions were somewhat entwined and the college, in surplus in the immediate aftermath of Maximilian's endowment, was expected to pass some of its money over to Watten. It was not long, however, before it again ran into debt, and turned to Maximilian for another donation, which he gave.

The Duke may have been generous, but it was not always easy getting the money from Munich. In 1641 the Provincial even considered stationing

---

1 He was also Archbishop-Elector of Cologne and held sundry other ecclesiastical titles though he was never consecrated bishop; indeed, he was never even ordained as a priest.

2 McCoog, *The Society of Jesus*, pp. 309-11. He calculates that the endowment was worth £1500 at the time, equal to approximately £300 million today, which seems an extraordinarily large amount of money.

a permanent representative in the city; the Provincial visited Maximilian's son and successor, Ferdinand Maria, in 1652 and the Rector of the English College in Rome did likewise the following year. Effort had to be put into finding other sources of income - in 1683 Catherine of Braganza, the wife of King Charles II, gave 200 scudi, as did Mary of Modena, the wife of the future King James II - but the endowment by Maximilian remained a mainstay of the College's often precarious finances. This was widely acknowledged, and at the time the Liège house was frequently known as the "Anglo-Bavarian" College.[1] Indeed, the coat of arms of the present College still recalls the link with the house of Wittelsbach - the family name of the Dukes of Bavaria - with its blue and white lozenges ("fusils askance" in heraldic parlance) of the Bavarian flag.[2]

One reason why the College was often chronically short of money was its sheer size. The property which had been purchased in 1613 consisted of a house and "ten arpents" of land: an "arpent" was an old French measure equivalent to approximately 59 metres or 64 yards, and the site has been calculated at approximately ten acres. It was set against the ramparts of the city, leading up to the citadel. One side was bounded by the rue des Jésuites Anglois (now simply called the rue des Anglais), and the other by the rue Montagne Ste Walburge. In what used to be the grounds of the College there is now a hospital. What the original building looked like can be seen from an engraving made in 1738 for a book entitled *Les Délices du Pais de Liège*. The main house faced the rue des Jésuites Anglois, and entering from the street the visitor was faced with a long staircase - Hubert Chadwick reckons a stair of some eighty steps[3] - before reaching the house. The main building had two wings, so forming three sides of a square, and rising up behind it four terraces, each one again reached by steps. The topmost of the terraces was given over

1 As, for instance, in the title of the book written by John Keynes and published by Henry Streel in 1685, dedicated to the then Duke of Bavaria on the occasion of his marriage, *Florus Anglo-Bavaricus*, to which reference will be made later.

2 The lozenges had originally been the escutcheon of the Counts of Bogen, a title the Wittelsbachs had acquired in 1247.

3 Chadwick, *St Omers*, p. 360. Keynes, in *Florus Anglo-Bavaricus* makes a point of saying there were seventy steps to the main door.

to the students for recreation; the other three appear from the engraving to have been gardens or orchards.[1]

On the highest terrace there was a building known as St Joseph's, which was used as an infirmary or an isolation unit in times of plague. But it also served as the base for an observatory: as will be seen, the Jesuits had a considerable interest in astronomy. In the late 1720s there was built, or perhaps rebuilt, a residence for "Juniors", that is, for scholastics in the first year after completing their noviceship.

One survival from the early days at Liège is the "Customs Book" - there is a copy in the Belgian Royal Archives.[2] Obviously, every community belonging to a religious order required its members to follow the rule of life laid down by the Order's Founder. However, different houses commonly had different ways of applying the rule and these local variations were recorded in what was called the "Customs Book". In Decree 90 of the seventh General Congregation of the Society, that which elected Mutius Vitelleschi in November 1615, it was laid down that the customs of each house should be preserved in writing, and not simply by oral tradition, hence the 1633 "Customs Book" which allows us some glimpse of the daily life of the Jesuit community at Liège.

The day began with uncomfortably early masses at 5.00 am, though it would seem the scholastics attended mass at 6.30, having been woken at 5.00 for an hour of meditation, beginning at 5.30. On major feast days, however,

1 "It certainly stands very airy, and pleasant and healthy", wrote the Rev. Theophilus Dorrington in his *Observations concerning the Present State of Religion in the Romish Church* (London, John Wyat, 1699) after a visit when he was "civilly and easily admitted, upon saying only that we were Englishmen, come out of curiosity to see the country". Dorrington's remarks were quoted in the *Stonyhurst Magazine*, no. VIII, December 1882, pp. 141-42. Not that he was particularly friendly to his hosts. As the entry on him in the *Oxford Dictionary of National Biography* notes, "After touring the continent, he wrote *Observations Concerning ... the Romish Church* (1698) to warn against harbouring its superstitious practices, to guard against divisive Jesuit influences, and to encourage protestants abroad". As to its being healthy, Edwards (*The Jesuits*, p. 49) notes that the number of novices increased after the move of the novitiate to Liège, partly because fewer of them died there than had died in Louvain.

2 Pierre Guérin, "Le coutumier des Jésuites anglais de Liège (1633)" *Bulletin de l'Institut archeologique Liégeois* t. C. (1988) pp. 215-223.

a community mass was celebrated around midday. Solemn, sung masses were held on such days, which included the most important occasions of the Church's calendar, such as Easter, Pentecost and Christmas, the feasts of the main saints of the Society, of Ignatius himself, Francis Xavier, Francis Borgia - in 1633 still ranked as a "Blessed" rather than a saint - and the patron saint of scholastics, Aloysius Gonzaga, also at that time still a "blessed".[1] There was also a solemn mass on the feast day of St Thomas Becket, the Archbishop of Canterbury, who, in English Catholic eyes, had been martyred for refusing to bow to the wishes of King Henry II and quite naturally, therefore, an iconic figure for recusants, especially recusant clergy.

Unlike all the religious orders founded before the Society of Jesus, Jesuits did not sing, or even recite, the divine office in common, the daily praying of which was an obligation on all clergy. At Liège they did so, however, on major feasts, when they also sang the litany of the saints (on other days the litanies were recited) at four in the afternoon. Solemn masses were followed by exposition of the Sacrament. It seems that outsiders were not permitted to attend these services unless they could not go elsewhere - presumably, in other words, they were servants in the house, or guests. Students were permitted to receive communion twice a week, which was rather more often than was customary at the time.

After mass came breakfast at 7.30 to 8.00 for scholastics (the lay brothers had theirs at 6.30). Classes followed during the morning and then lunch was at 11.00, except on Sundays and feast days when it was at 11.30. Supper was normally at 6.30 pm, but on days of abstinence (non meat-eating days) it was at 7.00 and days of fasting at 7.15. Meat seems to have constituted a substantial part of the community's diet. At the main meal - lunch - the meat was usually mutton, though beef was served twice a week. After Easter, however, and until 24th June (feast of John the Baptist) mutton was replaced by veal. Lunch consisted of soup, an hors d'oeuvre, the main (meat) course,

1 Luigi Gonzaga came from an aristocratic family and joined the Society in 1585. He died of the plague, contracted while tending victims of the plague in Rome, while still a student of theology. He was declared a saint in 1726. Francis Borgia, who was also of course a nobleman (see above, p. 4), was canonised in 1670.

and a dessert. There was beer to drink, which was rationed for scholastics, though not for priests. There was more food on major feasts, for guests, or when people were either leaving the community or being welcomed back. Wine was served at meals only at the whim of the superior. There was reading at meals, though frequently there were sermons, preached to the community as a means of teaching the students how to use a pulpit after they had been ordained priests. The sermons were either in English or in French. After lunch and supper there was a period of "recreation" - the one which followed supper always ended with litanies at 8.00 pm - when the students could mingle and talk. The timetable also allowed for sports, up on the top terrace. It was, as can be seen, a highly-regulated life, even down to clothing: summer clothing was to be put on at the beginning of May, then changed back at the end of September.

Classes began at 8.45 am. The subjects taught will be discussed below but, apart from academic topics - Scripture, for instance, was taught for half an hour a day except on Mondays, when students studied Hebrew instead - there were cases of conscience, problems in moral theology, discussed on Sundays before supper, and "controversies" were debated on Mondays before supper while there were "repetitions" each day, a form of tutorial, while on Fridays those studying philosophy, and on Saturdays the theologians, had what the Custom Book describes as "discussions" with each member of the year taking the lead once every three weeks. Though classes were suspended from 14th August (the vigil of Assumption) until 12th October for the summer vacation, this did not stop "repetitions" and other academic exercises, while at the beginning of September there were spiritual exercises: a retreat.

There were, of course, examinations. Minor ones were held around Easter, major public ones at the end of the fourth year of theology: they lasted for two and a half hours, and would in part determine what status a priest had within the Society. In fact the less academically gifted scholastics had already been separated out on to the "short" course, which was not short, but perhaps less intense. They were examined at the Feast of the Assumption (15th August) or thereabouts. The diaconate was received at beginning of Lent; ordination to the priesthood took place before Passion Sunday.

As can be seen from its date, the Customs Book did not begin with the College, which had begun in Liège a decade before it was printed. However, what it laid down would have been what was practised hitherto, so it is quite likely that it represents the way of life in the College more or less from its beginnings. Though by modern standards the timings seem a little too austere, a scholastic beginning his studies in the mid-twentieth century would have recognised the rule it enshrined as very similar to that by which he was expected to live. It does, however, lack any mention of "Blandykes". The school at St Omer, from which the English Province drew very many of its recruits, acquired a house at Blandecques, a small village on the river Aa, about three miles from St Omer itself, to serve as a "villa house", or holiday home. The property, about four acres in all, contained a house, an orchard, a garden and a fishpond, and was close to the river itself. Students and staff of the school visited Blandecques for recreation on a fairly regular basis, though how often is not clear. After the school moved to Stonyhurst there were monthly breaks from classes, always on Thursdays, which came to be known as "Blandykes" from the name of the village where the villa house had been.[1]

Though it was originally a holiday for the school, "Blandykes" were also enjoyed by scholastics.[2] At first at Liège, however, there was no villa house in the style of that at Blandecques. The Jesuits therefore attempted in February 1655 to buy a house and garden at Tilff, which they paid for in gold sovereigns, but in June the sale was challenged in the courts by a canon of Sainte- Croix at Liège, one Nicolas Simonis, apparently claiming that it was his by inheritance. The Jesuits were obliged to concede and abandoned their purchase - but they got their money back. In fact a villa house was rented in the 1650s and on and off until the 1670s. Then the ardently Catholic Lord Castlemaine, husband of Barbara Villiers, Charles II's mistress, who often stayed at Liège, provided the money for the acquisition of a house at Chèvremont, about five miles from Liège. There appears to have been an associated farm which produced a tiny income for the College. There was also a small vineyard. It became the custom for groups from the College to go there for ten days at

1 Chadwick, *St Omers*, pp. 116-17.

2 There was a magazine produced by scholastics entitled *Blandyke Papers*.

a time during the vacation period of August and September. Observing the strict separation of ages as was customary in the Society, those studying philosophy went first, then the theological students and finally their professors.

The Jesuits had built a shrine to the Virgin Mary at their villa house, as was the custom. For no very obvious reason the statue became the centre of pilgrimage, and because people came there to pray, a rough chapel was constructed around the shrine. There were two statues of the Virgin, one of wood brought there by the Jesuits and the other chiselled out of stone, regarded as miraculous, of Notre-Dame de Foy, which was put there by the local inhabitants. In 1697 the chapel was extended, perhaps as a thanksgiving after the troubles that had beset the region, and the statue began to be invoked as Our Lady of Mercy. The chapel gradually became acknowledged as the church of the nail-makers, a major industry in the area, and was formally recognised as such in June 1722.[1]

The University of Liège has a manuscript of the menus served to the community at their villa house in the Augusts of 1789 and 1791. For instance, on their arrival on 15th August 1789, the Feast of the Assumption, the community was served fresh fish and salted herring. The following day for lunch they had boiled beef, mutton chops and roast chicken. Cauliflower turned up on the menu quite often and there was the occasional pigeon paté. Rabbit served with onions featured occasionally and so did a choice (apparently) of hare or goose. Potatoes are mentioned and green beans, though these not frequently, and a couple of times during the community's stay they were served "mince pye". There were, alas, even "small birds" for the community supper. Students and staff, it would seem, did not go hungry.

1 In 1790, after the French Revolution and well after the Suppression of the Society, Chèvremont was attacked by radical nail makers from the neighbourhood but, as one John Laurenson recounts "Fabius like, we saved ourselves and our cellar by our cunctation. Shots were fired and the gate was damaged, but then money changed hands and the radicals went away". Cf. Holt *Chevremont*, p. 123. Quintus Fabius Maximus Verrucosus Cunctator (ca. 280 BC - 203 BC), was a general who led the Roman army during the second Punic War. Aware that he would be unable to defeat the invading Carthaginians in open battle, he used what would now be called guerrilla tactics: the eptithet "cunctator" means "the delayer" or, less kindly "the hesitater" - and when first bestowed it was not meant kindly.

If that is how they lived, what they studied is outlined by John Keynes in the *Florus Anglo-Bavaricus*. "Florus", which sounds as though it should mean "flower" but doesn't,[1] was the name of a first-century AD historian who produced an epitome of the history of Rome: Keynes's book is an epitome of the history of the English College. After giving some account of its foundation - he had obviously read the original documents and sometimes quotes at length - he goes on to talk of the virtues displayed by the greater number (he carefully does not say all!) of English Jesuits whereby they satisfied the requirements of the College's Serene Founder. He then writes of some of the more outstanding exemplars among the Jesuits, and their sufferings on the English mission, particularly during the Oates Plot, an account of which takes up the second half of the book.[2] There is only one fairly short chapter which gives an insight into what was taught, though there are other sources which give some indication, including a manuscript catalogue of the books in the main library ("bibliotheca major"). This document has only recently been discovered, wrongly catalogued, in the Royal Library at Brussels.[3] Professor Maurice Whitehead, in a note appended to the copy of the manuscript he donated to the Heythrop Library, suggests that it was in one of the packing cases accidentally left behind at Maastricht when the community had to return to England in 1794, as will be described later, seized by the French, and carried off to Paris (it has a stamp of the French Bibliothéque Nationale), then recovered from Paris by Brussels in 1815.

---

1 It also means "shining" in Latin, but was rarely used in this sense.

2 Titus Oates alleged there was a Catholic plot to assassinate King Charles II. The deed was to be carried out by English Jesuits, about 90 of whom were in the country at the time. As a consequence some Jesuits were executed, as well as a few Catholic laymen, and others died in prison. Eventually Oates's anti-Catholicism got the better of him and he accused the Duke of York, the future King James II, of treason and was himself gaoled. Nonetheless, in the aftermath of Oates's accusation Catholics were banned from sitting in either house of Parliament, a ban not removed until Catholic Emancipation in 1829.

3 Royal Library Mss 9773.

It lists some 7,000 titles,[1] categorised under 12 letters from A to O (there is no I or J). The first category is Scripture and Scripture commentaries, then come Ascetical works followed by Law, canon and civil. Section D is "Theologi Externi", a puzzling term until one comes to Section E: "Theologi Societatis Jesu": "externi" clearly means non-Jesuits. There is a section devoted to catechetics and a very long one labelled "Historica". Next comes "Humanistae" - it includes the Iliad, for example, and the writings of Juvenal. Section L is headed "Philosophici & Medici". There are indeed books on medicine and on what one might now call pharmacology but works on mechanics are also to be found there - and even the writings of the Jesuits' great adversary Voltaire. The next section is on Mathematics, including the writings of Galileo, Section N is on controversy, beginning with the works of Robert Bellarmine, and finally comes the "Libri Mixti" in section N.[2]

The catalogue is prefaced by "Regulations concerning the Library". Readers, other than professors, were to return books twice a year, and leave them for three days before borrowing them again. Titles of books borrowed and the date had to be written down and no one was supposed to take more books than he had immediate need of. "All must remember", says the 10th rule, "the old regulation, that no one is to go into the Library with a Light", which must have rather impeded use of the collection on winter evenings. The first rule is a surprising one: it seems to suggest that Jesuits could, with the

1 Whitehead thinks there may have been another volume of the manuscript, on the grounds that there are no musical works mentioned. I rather doubt this, because the manuscript ends with a category of "Libri Mixti", a sort of *omnium gatherum* of books for which no other place might be found in the classification - which makes it seem as though it is the last section. In his book *English Jesuit Education* (Farnham, Ashgate, 2013), pp. 136-42, Whitehead provides a longer description of the Mss catalogue. He believes that the catalogue includes only books acquired after the suppression of the Society in 1773 on the grounds that the property of the English Jesuits was sealed up on the instructions of the Prince-Bishop. I doubt, however, that as many as 7,000 titles could have been acquired in so short a space of time, and see no reason to believe that the "sealing up" remained in force. After all, they were also forbidden to engage in specifically Jesuit devotions but were soon doing so.

2 There is a similar catalogue of the main library (Bibliotheca Major) at the school at St Omer. It is laid out in a very similar fashion, though the St Omer catalogue is printed, the last volume known to have been produced (in 1753) by the press established in the school by Robert Persons, c. 1608, 1608 being the date of its first known publication.

Rector's permission, lend books from the Library to non-Jesuits, something that would not have been countenanced in later centuries.[1]

Theophilus Dorrington left a description of the Library: "We went through a large room where they hold their disputes, and from thence into the library, which is a long narrow room like a gallery. It was well filled with books, which looked as if they were well used and studied. I may say of this library, it is rather useful than fine. Over several partitions of shelves there was written at the top of the room, Libri Theologici, Libri Juridici, Libri Medici, Libri Mathematici, &c. Two divisions had a little lattice over them, and they were locked up. Over these was the title Libri Prohibiti. Among these, I could observe, was Cornelii Jansenii Augustinus, some of the works of the German Reformers, the Novum Testamentum Gallicum, which I suppose is that called the Mons Testament. I could not see the name of any English divine among these; but on the back of one of the prisoners there was pasted a paper on which was written Sermons; this was a thin folio".[2]

The *Florus* says that the theology to be taught is that of St Thomas Aquinas, as was required by the *Ratio Studiorum*. There were two professors assigned to teaching it. As has already been remarked[3], it was possible to diverge from Thomas, at least a little. One of these professors of theology, and perhaps also of Scripture, first at Louvain and later at Liège had been Andrew White. Despite his ability White was removed from his post in 1629 "because of his rigorously conservative adherence to Thomas Aquinas. According to a Jesuit catalogue for that year, White had an excellent intellect

1 The expression used is lending to "externs", a term Jesuits applied to those who were not members of the Society, though it might possibly mean someone who was not a member of the College. There is a slight hint that the rules were written before the Suppression of the Society in 1773: the example of how to enter details of a book in the borrowers' register gives as an example the date 'Jan. 25 1772".

2 For Dorrington, see above, p. 16 fn. 1.

3 Cf. above, p. 6.

and good judgement, but mediocre prudence".[1] The College's loss, however, became Maryland's gain, and White later became a notable missionary among the Native Americans. The *Florus* goes on to say that two more professors teach moral theology and polemics, or controversy. The text mentions specifically 'cases of conscience', in which a moral problem would be proposed, and through discussion a solution might be reached: Heythrop students at least up to the move to London in 1970 would have been familiar with such an approach, though not necessarily with the topics. A number of those discussed in 1682-83 are contained in Volume I of the Liège Manuscript Collection in the Archives at Georgetown University. Many relate directly to the situation in England. The first is on fasting: whether it is licit for an English Catholic to put meat before his guests, whether a Catholic in England can entertain a noble (but heretical) person in his house for reasons of friendship and humanity (many authorities are cited on the topic), whether it is permitted to a Catholic in England to eat meat when this is forbidden by the Church.

This was a particularly delicate subject for English Jesuits. Jasper Haywood, a skilled theologian and Hebraist, was one of the first members of the Society to arrive in England. He arrived in 1581 and was banished in 1585 but in the meantime he did what other Jesuits would have done: he attempted to implement the reforms of the Council of Trent though, under the reign of Queen Elizabeth I, its decrees had not been formally published. The traditional rites of Sarum, York, Canterbury and so on had imposed strict fasting regimes, and an additional abstinence from meat on Saturdays. Haywood declared these rules had been abrogated. He was told, however, that he was wrong and that the stricter regulations were still in force. Indeed, they remained so until 1777,

1 Thompson Cooper, "White, Andrew (1579-1656)", Rev. Thomas M. McCoog, *Oxford Dictionary of National Biography*, Oxford University Press, 2004; online edn, May 2007. [http://www.oxforddnb.com/view/article/29236, accessed 10 June 2013]. White was born in London in 1579 and was one of the first to join the noviceship in Louvain. He went to Maryland in 1633 and worked there for ten years, becoming remarkably proficient in at least two of the indigenous languages. He died, probably in Hampshire, in 1656.

some of them until 1830[1].

As all weddings in England had to take place before a Church of England minister, so marriage was also a problem. After fasting there follow some cases on matrimony, including whether it was permissible for a priest in England to bless the clandestine marriages of Catholics who are in an illicit relationship with a heretic. The next question is on baptism, followed by one on prohibited books - whether a priest in England can have in his library books by heretics. The next is on the so-called ("dicto") Anglican oath of allegiance. The text discusses the state of the question, and includes a version of the oath in the reign of Charles II. The remainder are mainly about priests in England, about saying the divine office, about the evening meal on fast days and on dispensations for eating meat on days of abstinence. More generally there are also controversies on the status of Councils of the Church.

At least until well into the twentieth century students of the College would also have been familiar with "polemics", a major part of the Liège curriculum for, as has been seen, the English Jesuits were given funding to study how heretics might be refuted. This was not limited to the study of controversy itself, the *Florus* notes, but each professor seized every opportunity presented by his own subject - including Scripture - to demonstrate how Protestants were mistaken.[2] The students took this seriously, the *Florus* says,

1 After completing this text I discovered that a series of cases discussed by Thomas Southwell had been edited by Peter Holmes and published as *Caroline Casuistry* (Woodbridge, The Boydell Press for the Catholic Record Society, 2012). They are very similar in style to the somewhat later - the "Caroline" refers to King Charles I not Charles II - manuscripts in the Georgetown collection, though from my cursory examination of the latter, Thomas Southwell seems to have been rather more of a rigorist.

2 The author of the *Florus* was himself a controversialist, in particular being a persistent critic of the Anglican theologian Edward Stillingfleet, the Bishop of Worcester. The first part of Volume II of the Georgetown Liège Manuscript Collection contains a discussion of Stillingfleet, and although no author is given the dates of the text (1683-84) suggest it might well have been Keynes. He was the author of, among other works, *A rational, compendious way to convince, without any dispute, all persons whatsoever, dissenting from the true religion* which was first published in English in London in 1674, then in a Latin translation at Liège in 1684 and finally in French, at St Omer, in 1688. Keynes served in many offices in the English Province, including that of Provincial, but he was also Prefect of Studies, and later Rector, at the English College in Liège, dying in 1697.

because controversy was not limited to the class room, but they discussed among themselves during their free time how they might lead both learned and unlearned out of their heretical beliefs. Surprisingly little time is spent on biblical languages. Hebrew was taught more intensively than Greek, and some of the scholastics on their own initiative studied other languages, such as Syriac, all with the aim, says *Florus*, of refuting heretics.

Examinations were oral - and in Latin - as they remained until the late 1950s and still for the most part remain oral in Roman colleges down to the present, if no longer in Latin. Apart from examinations there were academic exercises during which theses had to be defended. The process was medieval in origin: someone proposed a "thesis", a statement of a position, and this would then be attacked by opponents ("objicients") using Aristotelian logic.[1] This in turn required that the scholastics had already applied themselves to philosophy, and particularly to Dialectics. Again as the Florus indicates, they had spent three years under three professors studying "the peripatetics", in other words, the philosophy of Aristotle, just as the *Ratio Studiorum* required. Not that Keynes devotes much space to the studies - only a little over two pages - and, of that, scarcely any lines at all are devoted to what might now be understood as philosophy. Keynes goes on to talk far more about mathematics in its various branches, optics[2] and astronomy. Anything London's Royal Society can do, Keynes boasts, Liège's professors can also do - and better.[3] There are a good many books on mathematics, he notes, written by Jesuits, which have not been published, either because the Province could not afford it as it has from the beginning been beset by troubles and almost brought to its knees, or because there was a lack of patrons to underwrite the costs of the

1 Later known as "circles" they are described at greater length below, pp. 81 f.

2 It is no surprise, therefore, that the Heythrop Library owns a copy of Isaac Newton's *Optics*.

3 Opsomer notes ("Un foyer d'études") that after the publication of Newton's *Principia Mathematica* the professors at the college became enthusiastic Newtonians (unlike their counterparts at the University of Louvain) because they thought it accorded well with Aristotelian metaphysics.

battles.[1] But he seems to think that people might find it odd that so much time was given over to the study of mathematics and other sciences. These studies, he insists, are at the service of the sacred sciences, they are the means by which the Jesuits can gain access to learned men, and then, when they have their attention, talk to them about matters of faith.

The College professors were of course not unaware of the potential problems in treating of questions of science. Surviving manuscripts explain three different cosmological systems, those of Ptolemy, Tycho Brahe and Copernicus. The first the professors refuted, the second they either refuted or declared to be inadequate, the third is praised as the most widely accepted. They accept - how could they not after the condemnation of Galileo - that the Copernican system seemed to be in conflict with Scripture but, it was argued, it could be proposed as an hypothesis. As the Maryland-born Fr Joseph Semmes, professor of metaphysics and experimental physics at Liège and later at Stonyhurst, put it, it is not the role of Scripture to teach astronomy, that is why it uses the language of common sense.

The College was, perhaps, better known for its science than it was for its religion. One member of its staff was Francis (though he also called himself Thomas) Line[2] who was born, possibly in London, in 1595, who became novice in August 1623, was ordained priest in 1628 and took his final vows as a Jesuit in 1640. He was appointed the Professor of Mathematics and Hebrew in 1630, though it was in the former that he made his name. "Physics"

---

1 Opsomer points out ("Un foyer d'études") that while a number of manuscript treatises survive, there were at least a couple of printed books, *Trigonometria plana et sphaerica cum selectis ex Geometria et Astronomia problematis. Accedunt Sinuum canones, et ex Euclide Propositiones magis necessariae*, by James Gooden "in Collegio Anglorum Leodii Matheseos professore", published in Liège, Bronckart, 1704 and *Arithmetica methodice et succincte tradita Adiuncta ad Praxin Ratione* by Edward Slaughter "in Collegio Anglorum Leodii Matheseos quondam Professore". The edition seen by Opsomer is undated, and published in Cologne by Christian Schorn, apparently in 1767, but the first edition was 1702 and there was another in 1725: Slaughter, who had been born in Herefordshire in 1655, as well as mathematics also taught Hebrew (and as has been noted wrote a highly successful grammar thereof) and theology. He died at Liège in 1729.

2 This section is heavily dependent on Francis Line *An Exiled English Scientist, 1595-1675*, by Conor Reilly (Rome: Institutum Historicum S.I., 1969).

was also part of his remit. It was at the time understood in the Aristotelian sense, that is to say dealing with the general principles of natural things, especially things in motion, and was therefore part of philosophy[1]. He based his teaching on commentaries on Aristotle's Physics, especially the widely-used *Commentarium Conimbricensis Societatis Jesu in Octo Libros Physicorum Aristotelis* by Jesuits of Coimbra in Portugal.

Line was teaching at Liège at the height of the controversy over Galileo's espousal of the Copernican theory - and at the time it was in effect only a theory - that the world moved around the sun rather than vice versa: Galileo was finally condemned by the Roman Inquisition in June 1633 and committed to house arrest for the rest of his life. Line himself was a close friend of one of Galileo's most convinced disciples. He became indirectly embroiled in the controversy because another of Galileo's supporters believed, wrongly, that a water clock which Line had constructed in the gardens of the College might provide proof of the validity of Galileo's teaching.[2]

Line was famous for his clocks. Dorrington[3] describes "the blind man's dial, because a blind man having once learned the order of the numbers at the end of the lines, might by feeling find what time of day it is, thus: the hour lines, at which the figures were set, were little flat bars of iron; and a glass globe full of water was so set between it and the sun as to contract the burning point successively, according to the sun's motion upon these lines; this burning point would be sensible to his finger, and he would thereby know the time of the day. In a concave dial, which had wires laid over it to make the shadow, and the hour lines meeting all in one centre, they had set a little picture of our Saviour, with His finger at that centre, and a motto, as proceeding

1 Cf. Sir Isaac Newton, Query 31: "To derive from the natural phenomena two or three general principles of motion, and then to explain how the properties and actions of all material things result from these manifest principles - would be a great progress in philosophy indeed", quoted Zeljko Marković, "Boscovich's *Theoria*" in *Roger Joseph Boscovich*, edited by Lancelot Law Whyte (London, Allen and Unwin, 1961), p. 131.

2 The water clock became well known, and the Rome-based Jesuit polymath, Athanasius Kirchner, claimed to have discovered Line's "secret" and built a similar device which he described in his *Magnes sive de Arte Magnetica* (Rome, 1641).

3 Cf.p.16fn1.

from Him, in these words, 'Haec est hora tua'": "This is your hour".

Another of Line's inventions, a pyramidal sundial, caught the eye of Prince Charles, the future King Charles II, when he visited the College and was entertained to lunch. Line had returned to England around the beginning of 1658 - to the irritation of some of his colleagues in the College who complained to the Jesuit General in Rome - and spent a number of years working on the mission, before in 1670 returning to his post at Liège where he died in November 1675. While he was in England, Charles, now restored to the throne, asked him to replace the sundial in the gardens of Whitehall Palace. Line's installation was a large structure with a number of different dials so that, as he put it, "the hours according to the Jewish, Babylonian, Italian [possibly the Gregorian calendar?] and astronomical ways of reckoning" might be read,[1] but, like the dial in the College gardens, it also included one dial which would enable a blind person to tell the time. This was unveiled in July 1669, but it had only stood in the gardens for a few years when it was badly damaged by an inebriated earl, and was subsequently removed. Line wrote about it in a book published in Liège in 1673, but even then, before the depravations of the drunken Lord Rochester, it had suffered damage from the frosts of an English winter.

Francis Line, who seems to have been an argumentative sort of person, engaged in a number of controversies while in England. A Belgian Jesuit claimed he had worked out a formula by which the area of a circle would be transformed into the area of a square ("squaring the circle"), and would not listen to evidence to the contrary. The Belgian engaged in acrimonious controversy with his critics, and Line thought he ought to be stopped. He therefore wrote to the Jesuit General, Goswin Nickel, asking him to intervene. Nickel not surprisingly wrote back saying he had more pressing things to think about than solving mathematical problems.[2] Thomas White, a secular priest whom Line had met, also wrote a treatise claiming to be able to solve the circle/square problem. His calculations contained some fundamental errors, and this Line pointed out in *De Pseudo-Quadratura Circuli Dom Thoma Viti*,

1 Quoted by Reilly, *An Exiled English Scientist*, p. 99.

2 Reilly, *An Exiled English Scientist*, p. 39.

which was followed by a translation, *Refutation of the Attempt to Square the Circle*. Both appeared in London, where the author was at this time.

Line returned to England late in 1657 or early the following year. It seems possible he went at the request of some nobleman. In 1661 he dedicated his *De corporum inseparabilitate* to Henry Pierrepoint, the Marquis of Dorchester, who was later an FRS (the Royal Society received its charter a year later). This book was a criticism, largely from an *a priori* stance based upon Line's Aristotelian principles, of Robert Boyle's experiments which had shown that air exerted pressure and that it was possible to create a vacuum. (In his rejection of Boyle, Line had the unlikely support of Thomas Hobbes.) In the second edition of his *New Experiments* Boyle included an appendix in answer to Line: "This opinion [i.e., that of Line] as to the main, being approved by many eminent scholars, especially of that most learned order of the Jesuits (to whom perhaps its congruity to some articles of their religion chiefly recommends it) I was the more willing to pay them that respect, as not to dissent from persons, divers of whom for their eminence in mathematics and other learnings I much esteem, without showing that I do it not but upon considerations that I think weighty". Boyle's respectful attitude to the Society was all the more surprising because he was close to the French Jansenists who were the Society's great adversaries, especially as regards the Jesuits' teaching on morality which they regarded as far too lax. It was in answering Line, incidentally, that Boyle formulated what has ever since been called "Boyle's Law".[1]

Line had not yet done with scientific controversy. In 1672 Newton published a paper on optics - his first on the subject - in the recently established *Philosophical Transactions of the Royal Society.* He argued that white light was made up of different colours, which he demonstrated by passing them through a prism. This was criticised by a Jesuit who taught at the College of Clermont in Paris, Ignace Gaston Pardies. After an exchange of letters with Newton, Pardies came to accept that Newton's experimental method had proved correct, but he died, of a fever caught while tending prisoners in Paris,

1 Reilly, *An Exiled English Scientist*, p. 72

at the age of 37. Line thought Pardies had given in too soon to Newton, and there was another exchange of letters in the pages of the *Transactions*, in the course of which Line, who had replicated Newton's experiments, eventually asserted that Newton's experiments with the prism could not possibly have yielded the results which Newton claimed. The controversy was still underway when Line died. However, the debate was promptly reopened by a layman (they had been allowed into the College in 1672), writing under a pseudonym. He demanded that Newton's experiment with the prism should be conducted at the Royal Society itself. This was done in April 1676: the results confirmed Newton's findings. But now Anthony Lucas SJ, Line's successor at Liège as Professor of Mathematics, entered the fray. He had himself conducted the experiments and in some ways his results supported Newton against Line, but in other respects, he insisted, the results still differed. The differences could be accounted for, he suggested, by the different types of glass that were used in the prisms. Newton, however, ruled out that possibility, believing that any material through which light could pass would yield the same results - and in this case it was Newton who was wrong. Letters went to and fro between Lucas and Newton until 1678, though nothing was printed in the *Transactions* after 1676.[1]

Thomas Hildeyard was, like Line, a clockmaker. Born in London in 1690 and - inevitably - educated at St Omer, he was only briefly a member of the College staff at Liège, twice in fact, from 1718 to 1720 and then again from 1723 to 1726, teaching philosophy, theology and mathematics. During his second period at the College he published a book[2] describing his "astronomical" clock with four faces, which showed the position of the planets and the signs of the Zodiac as well as the times of sunrise and sunset and many other similar details. According to Opsomer, quoting Pierre Guérin,[3] the clock survives, and is now to be found in the study of the King of Spain at the

1 See also, C. Reilly, "A catalogue of Jesuitica in the Philosophical Transactions of the Royal Society of London (1665-1715)", *Archivum Historicum Societatis Iesu 27* (1958), pp. 339-62.

2 *Descriptio horologii recens inventi a R.P. Thoma HILDEYARD Societatis Jesu olim Matheseos nunc Theologiae professore in Collegio Anglicano Leodii*, Liège, G. Barnabé, 1725.

3 Opsomer, "Un foyer d'études"; P. Guérin and André Thiry, "Horologe astronomiquc liègeoise dans le bureau du roi d'Espagnc" in *Horlogerie ancienne. Revue de l'Association Française*, 49 (2001), pp. 65-79.

Zarzuela Palace, the official residence of the Spanish monarch located on the outskirts of Madrid. He was, however, perhaps more famous for having been the first person on the continent of Europe to build the steam engine which had been designed in England by Thomas Newcomen. The story sounds a little cloak-and-dagger-ish. It seems that a Swiss colonel had passed on to a Liège entrepreneur the plans of the engine, but the details were recounted in English. Hildeyard, who was renowned for his engineering skills, was asked to translate, but went further, and built a working model of Newcomen's invention which seems to have been exhibited in the College Library. Hildeyard returned to the English mission in 1726, and spent most of the rest of his life - he died in 1746 - as a chaplain at Rotherwas near Hereford.

Clocks seem to have been something of a College speciality. Among the Georgetown collection of Liège manuscripts is one neatly bound in the form of a slim book, "Tractatus de Horographia, Sphaerae armillaris &quorundam in Astronomia Praeliminalia Explicatio". The text begins with the distinctly pre-Copernican words "Terra in centro firmamentum stat immobilis", "The earth stands immoveable in the centre of the universe". The author explains terms used in astronomy, including the signs of the zodiac. He goes on to discuss how different types of clock are made, including a sun dial ("horologus solare") for someone who is blind. At the end there are a number of hand-drawn mathematical diagrams showing the positions of the signs of the zodiac. At the bottom of the final page are the words "ex dono autoris Edv Slaughter 18 Janij an 1725 Leodij": "The gift of the author, Edward Slaughter, 18 January 1725 at Liège".

Another English Jesuit mathematician of the time, though someone of a rather different character to the combative Line, the mechanical Hildeyard or the polymath Slaughter, was Christopher Maire.[1] Maire, who was born in 1697, like others of his Durham family went to school at St Omer and entered the Society at Watten in 1715 and eventually went to study philosophy and theology at the Liège College, returning to teach there in the mid-1730s before

1 Geoffrey Holt "*An Able Mathematician*": Christopher Maire" in *Recusant History* vol. xx (1991), pp. 497-502.

being called to Rome to serve as the rector of the English College. In Rome he became acquainted with the Dubrovnik-born Jesuit, generally known in the anglicised version of his name as Roger Boscovich, an "astronomer, mathematician, physicist, geodesist, hydrographer, philosopher and poet".[1] He was in addition an admirer of Newton, who was in part the inspiration for Boscovich's *Theoria* (in effect, a theory of everything but of which Maire was somewhat sceptical), and a Fellow of the Royal Society. One of the great scientific issues of the day was the precise shape of the earth, which Newton had argued was an ellipsoid, that is to say, flattened at the poles. Boscovich was invited to join an expedition to Brazil to prepare an accurate map, but Pope Benedict XIV persuaded him to prepare accurate maps of the Papal States instead and, in the process, by calculating the arc of the meridian, to contribute towards a determination of the earth's shape. He was joined in this enterprise, which lasted from 1750 to 1752, by Christopher Maire, of whom Boscovich had a high opinion as a very able mathematician and an accurate observer who had published on astronomy, and had worked out the measurements of London's St Paul's Cathedral. Maire was no newcomer to map-making. He had honed his skills first on his home county of Durham, producing a map of the County Palatine when he was only some fourteen years old, and then making one of the earliest detailed plans of Liège, which was published in that city in 1746.[2] The report by Boscovich and Maire, with the most careful maps to date of the Papal States, published in Latin in Rome in 1755 and later translated into French, was in five parts. Maire wrote parts two and three. Parts one and four and five are by Boscovich and are largely theoretical but Maire's contribution was to print his calculations and, in part three, to produce the map. In the process they had determined, more accurately than had been done hitherto, the height of the poles.[3]

After this expedition, which, to facilitate triangulation, involved climbing not just Italian mountains but scaling the cupolas of Italian churches, apparently to the amazement, and distress, of onlookers who thought it sacrilege,

1 Elizabeth Hill, "Roger Boscovich: A biographical essay", in *Roger Joseph Boscovich*, edited by Lancelot Law Whyte (London, Allen and Unwin, 1961), pp. 17-111, quotation at p. 17.

2 Cf. Whitehead, *An English Jesuit Edcation*, p. 121.

3 Hill, Boscovich, p. 45.

Maire went back to a relatively quiet life at Rome's English College, now no longer serving as its Rector. He later returned briefly to St Omer, and died at the Jesuit house in Ghent in 1767.

It may seem odd that the three Jesuits whose careers have been mentioned above are scientists. The College at Liège was, after all, primarily a College of philosophy and theology. It has to be remembered that philosophy and science were in the minds of the learned of the day closely related. There were nonetheless members of the College staff who were theologians, such as John Floyd (1572-1649), who served for a time as Rector when the house was in Louvain or Thomas Southwell (1592-1637), who taught at Liège and published in 1628 at Antwerp *Regula viva, seu, Analysis Fidei in Dei per Ecclesiam*. At the time of his death he was preparing a commentary on the *Summa Theologiae* of St Thomas Aquinas[1]. Writers like Floyd, however, or John Keynes, mentioned earlier as one of the authors of *Florus Anglo-Bavaricus*, tended to be religious controversialists, as perhaps the age demanded,[2] and that remained true at least to the end of the seventeenth century and into the early years of the eighteenth, carried on by men such as William Darrell and Lewis Sabran.

Sabran was to play a rather unusual role in Liège. In the mid-seventeenth century there arose in France a Catholic reform movement taking its inspiration from a work on St Augustine called, precisely, *Augustinus*, by Cornelius Jansen, the bishop of Ypres. The book was not published until 1640, after Jansen's death, and was promptly condemned by the Inquisition for, among other things, its apparently Calvinist doctrine on predestination. The controversy went on well into the eighteenth century but it was more than a theological debate: there arose out of it an extremely rigorist spirituality and, more specifically, an attack on the moral teaching of the Society of Jesus. Jansenists regarded Jesuit moral theology as far too lax, and said so, most particularly in Blaise Pascal's devastating *Lettres Provinciales* of 1656, a

1 For Thomas Southwell, one of three Jesuit brothers whose real name was Bacon, see below, p.24 fn1.

2 For Floyd's writings, see the index to Peter Milward, *Religious Controversies of the Jacobean Age: A Survey of Printed Sources* (London, Scolar Press, 1970), p. 230

criticism of Jesuit casuistry. English Jesuits seem on the whole to have avoided public debate about Jansenism though Martin Grene, who was a professor in the College from 1641 to 1653, translated from the French, and adapted for English readers, *An answer to the Provincial Letters published by the Jansenists* (Paris, 1659) and went on to write *An Account of the Jesuits Life and Doctrine* (London 1661). The casuistry which Pascal so brilliantly satirised is simply the method of dealing with people's moral problems or "cases". In common parlance, however, it has come to mean splitting hairs and exactly that figured as part of Pascal's critique. As has been noted above,[1] dealing with cases of conscience was an important part of Jesuit theological education: the just-mentioned William Darrell, for instance, was for a time Professor of Casuistry at Liège as well as serving as Rector between 1708 and 1712.

The professors at the episcopal seminary in Liègc, all of whom had been educated at the University of Louvain, were deeply imbued with Jansenism, and as a consequence all the clergy of the diocese were extremely rigorist, laying heavy penances on those who came to them to confess, and all too readily refusing their penitents absolution. At the end of 1698 the Rector of the seminary died and the Prince-Bishop, Josef Clemens of Bavaria, replaced him not with a diocesan priest but with Lewis Sabran in an effort to rid the seminary of Jansenism. Sabran had hitherto led a somewhat extraordinary life. He was the son of the Marquis de Sabran, in the Provençal nobility, who had been ambassador to the court of St James and married an English wife. After attending the College at St Omer he joined the Society, and went through the normal training, including a period at Liège. When James II came to the throne he became a royal chaplain and afterwards chaplain to the infant Prince of Wales. After the 1688 revolution he returned to the continent. He served in a number of offices in the Society before being selected, with permission of the General, to take over the Liège seminary. This was not an unusual step: a number of diocesan seminaries in France at this period were being run by Jesuits, possibly for the same reason that Sabran had been chosen, because of the Society's anti-Jansenist stance.

Sabran himself was not distinguished as a theologian though, while

1 See above p. 24.

at the court of James II, he had engaged in controversy with an Anglican divine and had taught moral theology at the English College in Liège, as well as acting as the students' spiritual director. At the episcopal seminary he was assisted by Robert Henry Stephens. Stephens took over the presidency when Sabran was made Provincial in 1705, and remained in that post until his death in 1723, at which point the presidency reverted to the diocesan clergy. Stephens, who had been born in Liège,[1] was rather more of a theologian than Sabran and wrote four anti-Jansenist works.

There were a number of other Jesuits on the seminary staff, one of whom, James Gooden, was, like Maire, also a noted mathematician. But it was Stephens who aroused the most hostility among the clergy of the seminary. In 1702 a book was published, presumably at Liège though no place of publication is given, entitled *Specimen doctrinae a Jesuitis in seminario Leodiensi Traditae Tribus capitibus exhibitum* ["Example of the teaching delivered by the Jesuits in the seminary of Liège Expounded in Three Chapters"].[2] The first paragraph says that the author(s?) is taking as a starting point that golden rule of St Augustine: "Love the individuals, but slay their errors". The first chapter attacks Sabran and Edward Slaughter, but especially Sabran, from a Jansenist perspective for not being sufficiently rigorist on, for example, contrition and attrition. Sabran is clearly a probabilist,[3] and the author does not approve. He

1 A number of Liège-born men joined the English province, though mainly as lay brothers rather than, like Stephens, as priests.

2 The full title is: *Specimen doctrinae a Jesuitis in seminario Leodiensi Traditae Tribus capitibus exhibitum: Primo notantur corruptelae in Doctrina Morum & Fidei; Secondo injuriae in D. Augustinum; Tertio contumeliae in Augustinianos, Thomistas, Scotistas, adeoque in Ordines Religiosos, Universitates Catholicas & optimos quosque Theologos* ["Example of the teaching delivered by the Jesuits in the seminary of Liège Expounded in Three Chapters: In the first are noted perversions in the teaching on morals and faith; in the second injustices done to Augustine; in the third the abuses against Augustinians, Thomists, Scotists and against religious orders, Catholic universities and other excellent theologians"].

3 Probabilism, adhered to, for the most part, by members of the Society of Jesus, was the view that in case of conscience one might follow a probable opinion as to the rightness or wrongness of an action, even if there was a more probable opinion to the contrary. This may seem paradoxical, but it is derived from the simple premise that a law which lays down an obligation must be clear, and if there is any doubt, then the balance falls in favour of the freedom of the individual, who may act as he or she feels appropriate.

then goes on to attack Stephens for being a probabilist and also for his teaching on murder, taken from one of the disputations over which he presided at the seminary on 3rd October 1699. Stephens comes in for a great deal of criticism because his views, the author asserts, time after time contradict those of the "Clerus Gallicanus". Most of the book is effectively taken up with an attack on Stephens, who in turn is accused of attacking Augustinians, Thomists (as the book's title alleges) but especially, in the last chapter, for having attacked the Jansenists Antoine Arnauld and Blaise Pascal.[1]

There is a somewhat different account of the affair of the seminary recounted by the eminent historian of Jansenism, Louis Ceyssens. According to his source,[2] the English Jesuits had long wanted to teach courses that were open to the public, but could not because of the opposition of the University of Louvain.[3] They therefore set their eyes on the seminary and, to undermine the regime, they selected quotations from the writings of one of the professors there and sent them off to the Roman Inquisition. The Inquisition, however, found nothing heterodox. When in 1698 the Rector of the seminary fell ill, those who should have been responsible for electing his successor were blocked from doing so, and one of those who prevented them proceeding with the election (the source does not say how) was a brother of the then Rector of the English College.

The seminary professors did not readily accede to Sabran's appointment. Three of them together with the former President appealed to Rome, and the University of Louvain appealed to the agreement of 1614 which in 1639 had been endorsed by the Cardinal-Infante. So it fell to Maximilian-Emanuel, the

1 In Volume 8 of the Liège Manuscript Collection in Georgetown University Library there are on pp. 517- 535: *Propositiones Damnatae ab Alexandro VII* - 45 condemned propositions taken from Jansenist writings, followed by *Propositiones Damnatae ab Innocent XI* - 65 of them - and *Propositiones Damnatae ab Alexandro VIII* - 31 of them. These are in turn followed by a list of the propositions of Baius condemned by Pius V, Gregory XIII and Urban VIII, 79 of them: Baius (1513-89) was a professor at, and sometime Rector of, the University of Louvain. Like Jansenius, on Augustine's doctrine of grace he held views regarded as heterodox.

2 L. Ceyssens, "L'Affaire du Seminaire de Liège d'apres l'historien janseniste Gabriel du Pac de Bellegarde 1786" in *Annuaire d'histoire Liègoise* 15, 1947, pp. 663-762. Ceyssens records du Pac's account almost without comment.

3 See above, p. 12.

Elector of Bavaria, to decide the issue as Governor-General of the Spanish Netherlands. He was also, as has been seen, brother of the Prince-Bishop, Joseph Clement, who had made the appointment. The University's argument was that, in the act of 9th December 1425 by which the University had been erected, Pope Martin V had given it a monopoly of higher education over the region - which included Liège because at the time of its foundation Louvain lay within the Liège diocese. The Prince-Bishop, on the other hand, pointed out to his brother that the Council of Trent gave him complete authority over his seminary as the diocesan ordinary. He therefore sent the Vicar General with soldiers (under the command of a Lutheran officer!) to enter the seminary by force, breaking down doors so that the Vicar General could enter and Lewis Sabran be formally invested with his office of President. In the War of Spanish Succession, however, Josef Clemens chose the wrong side and in 1702 he was driven from his bishopric, though he was restored in 1714. It may have been his fall from grace that led to Sabran's retirement from the presidency, he being regarded by the incoming, albeit (as it turned out) temporary, imperial governor as having been too close to the exiled bishop.

The controversy over the presidency of the episcopal seminary was not, however, the whole story. It became evident that there was a considerable degree of antagonism towards the English Jesuits from the diocesan priests and not just because of their alleged laxity in the confessional: the priests even, they alleged, sometimes absolved people from excommunications without asking permission of a higher authority. They also accused the Jesuits of allowing their students too great a degree of freedom. There was a notable lack of discipline among them, even late-night drinking, and far too much noise. The bishop tut-tutted, but the English Jesuits remained in charge until Stephens's death. However, even while the English Jesuits were in charge, some students still wished to attend the English College rather than the seminary and continued to do so. In 1726, for example, after having studied at the Walloon Jesuit College in Liège, one young man asked, and was given, permission to study philosophy with the English Jesuits on condition that he followed the same rules as those in the seminary. A couple of years later two philosophy professors at the seminary petitioned the Prince-Bishop because, they said, the English Jesuits were accepting anyone into their College even if they did not have permission of the Bishop's Privy Council. This, argued the professors, was contrary to the privileges granted to the seminary by the Bishop's illustrious predecessors. Moreover, those attending the English College were not keeping the rules they would be required to observe in the seminary, such as attending catechism each Sunday, hearing mass and from time to time going to communion, going out in their cloaks and being properly dressed. Because of these freedoms enjoyed by the students at the English College, they went on, more and more men were abandoning the seminary for the College. They wanted the Bishop to forbid the English Jesuits from accepting students unless they had received written permission of the Bishop's Privy Council which, they thought, should rarely be granted. Such students who were granted it, they went on, ought to be required to live by the seminary rules.

The priests' protests did not seem to make much difference to the reputation of the English College among the young men of Liège. But was the reputation justified? It was an issue on which Bishop John Carroll held strong views. Carroll was born in Upper Marlboro, Maryland in 1735 and was sent by his parents to study at St Omer, subsequently joining the Jesuits and being ordained at Liège in 1769. He taught briefly at Bruges, where the St Omer's college had been forced to move, before being asked to accompany Charles Philip, afterwards the 16th Baron Stourton, on the Grand Tour. The Tour began in 1771 and lasted for almost two years, ending on the eve of the Suppression of the Society of Jesus - of which more later. After the Suppression, Carroll went first to England and then almost immediately returned home to work as a missionary in Maryland and Virginia. Technically the clergy in colonial Maryland fell under the jurisdiction of the Vicar Apostolic of the London District, at the time the very distinguished Bishop Richard Challoner. But this was an anomalous situation: in 1776 the United States became an independent country yet its Catholic clergy were still answerable to the representative, as it might seem, of the colonial power. Challoner's successor - Challoner himself died in 1781 - therefore refused to take on the responsibility, and Carroll was appointed superior of the mission in 1784, with quasi-episcopal powers. Five years later John Carroll was elected by an almost unanimous vote of the clergy to be Bishop of Baltimore. He was ordained bishop in England, in the chapel of the Welds of Lulworth, and served as Bishop, and from 1808 as Archbishop, of Baltimore until his death in that city in 1815.[1]

Carroll did not rejoin the restored English Province: after he became a bishop this was not an option open to him even had he wished to do so. Nevertheless he remained on close terms with many of his former colleagues, as his letters indicate, and closely followed their fortunes individually, and that of the Liège community as a whole. For instance, he wrote from Baltimore to Francis Beeston in March 1788, "The experience of a Liège education, at the advanced price of £40 per ann:[2] for young ecclesiastics renders it impracticable for any Americans to profit by that excellent institution [the Liège College]; and even that (without a restoration of the Society) is liable to degeneracy".[3] Some years later, however, he was less than complimentary about "that excellent institution". Writing to his very good friend Charles Plowden, whom he tried to recruit as president of what was eventually to become Georgetown University, he commented in 1803:

> "Did I not mention to you in a former letter, that on reading Mr. Butlers *Horae bibliae*, or his life of his uncle or his life of his uncle Alban, I was pleased to find the Gentlemen of your house called upon to exercise themselves in some beneficial works, and employ their

1 The major work on John Carroll is the two-volume study by Peter Guilday, *The Life and Times of John Carroll* (New York, The Encyclopedia Pres, 1922). Annabelle Melville's *John Carroll of Baltimore* (New York: Charles Scribner, 1955) is a good deal shorter, and corrects some of Guilday's errors. But see also Thomas O'Brien Hanley (ed.), *The John Carroll Papers* (Notre Dame: University of Notre Dame Press, c. 1976), 3 vols., to which reference will be made in what follows.

2 The sum is odd. Only a year before the abrasive Fr John Ashton, who had been appointed the financial controller for the ex-Jesuits in America, had written to William Strickland in London quoting a much smaller figure: "Tho' I think ye pension of 25 guineas much higher than would be required in many other ecclesiastical seminaries, yet on ye whole I prefer Liège because we know that they will there receive ye same principles & habits of virtue in which ye members of ye Society were trained & they will have ye advantage of learning the English language" (Quoted by Geoffrey Holt, *William Strickland and the Restored Jesuits* (London, Society of Jesus, 1988), pp. 80-81. A number of priests had been sent from Liège to the Maryland mission, kitted out at the expense of the English ex-Jesuits: there had been some twenty English Province priests in America at the time of the Suppression (Holt, *William Strickland*, p. 75).

3 Hanley, *The John Carroll Papers*, p. 292.

talents and learning in the cause of literature and religion? It must be owned, that for more than a century, we have been greatly eclipsed by the Gentlemen of Doway; witness Hawarden, Manning, Walton, Challenor, Butler, & now Milner & Coombs[1]. Sometimes I have reflected on the causes of it, & those which I suggested to myself, operate, it is hoped, no longer at present. It seemed to me that at Liège far from encouraging young men to extend the circle of their knowledge, the heads of the College esteemed no merit but that of the study of their dictates. The little of Greek that had been learned at S. Omer or Bruges, was suffered to perish; the Hebrew lesson was a mere mockery; even the cultivation of Latin elegance was thrown aside; and as to our native language, there was scarcely a book of it in the library worthy of being studied. No modern author of any science or in any languagc was introduced into it. Thus genius and talent were cramped, & a habit of inapplication was acquired, which few escaped. But, by the removal to England, it will be made necessary to go deeper into the recesses of science: and there can be no doubt, but this will be

1 Charles Butler (1750-1832), was, like all those mentioned here by Carroll, educated at the English College at Douai by secular clergy but, unlike the others, remained a layman. He was a lawyer, a political writer, a commentator on the Scriptures, and a controversialist in the intra-Catholic debates at the end of the 18th century. His uncle Alban Butler (1709-1773) compiled the well-known *Lives of the Saints* which, though in a completely revised version, still bears his name: there is a copy of the original four volumes in the Heythrop Library. Alban Butler not only studied but went on to teach at Douai and became its president. He also became president of the school at St Omer after the expulsion of the Jesuits. John Milner, 1752-1826 and from 1803 Vicar Apostolic of the Midland district, was the liberal Charles Butler's main adversary. Milner's best known work, *The End of Religious Controversy*, was published after the date of Carroll's letter. Edward Hawarden (1662-1735) had been Professor of Theology at Douai, and was much admired by Milner both as a theologian and a controversialist. Robert Manning (1655-1731) was best known for his *England's Conversion and Reformation Compared* which was regarded as seditious by the government, and was seized. Edward Walton (1715-1780) taught philosophy and theology at Douai before returning to England and from 1769 was Vicar Apostolic of the Northern District. He is unrecorded as an author. Richard Challoner (1691-1781) was from 1758 Vicar Apostolic of the London District and is perhaps nowadays the most admired of all those mentioned. He produced more than 60 works, many of them of controversy, but is chiefly remembered for his prayer book, *The Garden of the Soul*, which remained a staple of English Catholic devotional life well into the twentieth century. William Henry Coombes (1767-1850) taught theology at Douai and then in England.

> encouraged to the utmost. I long to hear of the revival of that spirit amongst the descendants of the Society, which shone forth in its first ages, & still exists in the Constitutions of S. Ignatius".[1]

These were views which Charles Plowden probably shared, though in a letter to Charles Brooke written about 1812 he restricts his criticism of the management of the college at Liège to the devastation - as he saw it - wreaked in the garden.[2]

In the final years of the existence of Liège as a Jesuit College, Thomas Ellerker was teaching there. According to George Oliver[3], Ellerker was "one of the ablest professors of theology that the English province ever produced". Oliver cites as evidence his *de Incarnatione*, which he describes as "Ellerker's *chef oeuvre*", but that work of only 80 pages, together with the 248-page *Tractatus theologicus de Jure et Justitia*, completed in 1767, never appeared in print. Both survive in a few copies only in manuscript form, a fact which rather lends weight to John Carroll's criticisms[4].

1 Hanley, *The John Carroll Papers*, vol. II, p. 409.

2 Letter quoted Whitehead, *English Jesuit Education*, p. 126, footnote 38.

3 *Collections towards illustrating the Biography of the Scotch, English and Irish Members S.J.* (Exeter, W. C. Featherstone, 1838), p. 70. For Oliver himself, see Geoffrey Holt, "George Oliver, Antiquary, from his letters" in *Transactions of the Devonshire Association for the Advancement of Science*, 119 (1987), pp. 53-65.

4 On Ellerker, see Geoffrey Holt, "Thomas Ellerker S.J., A Theologian from County Durham" in *Northern Catholic History*, no. 43 (2002), pp. 31-38.

THE SUPPRESSION, 1773

John Henry Newman once remarked that the suppression of the Society of Jesus was "one of the most mysterious matters in the history of the Church".[1] As Jonathan Wright has commented, "we must abandon the notion of a single, over-arching explanation"[2] of it. There were different reasons in different parts of the world, and, as will be seen, differing consequences in different places.

As John Carroll took his young charges around Europe he became increasingly aware of the threat to the very existence of the Society of Jesus. This was particularly so when he eventually arrived in Rome. He therefore wrote worried letters to his community at Bruges in the Austrian Netherlands, whither the St Omer College had been forced to migrate after the Parlement of Paris had decreed the abolition of the Jesuits in the regions under their control, and to friends in Liège.[3] Pope Clement XIII had done all he could to stem the rising tide of hostility, but after his death in 1762 he was replaced by the Franciscan Cardinal Lorenzo Ganganelli who became Pope Clement XIV. It has been much debated whether Ganganelli achieved the papacy by promising to take action against the Society, but there is no clear evidence one way or the other. Take action he did, however, and on 21st July 1773 he issued a Brief, *Dominus ac Redemptor*, suppressing the Society of Jesus.

The Brief praises the past history of the Jesuits - it could hardly do otherwise, given that its Founder had been declared a Saint - but goes on to provide precedents for popes abolishing religious orders and talks about the failings demonstrated by the Society, the controversies it had aroused and the, to his mind, excessive privileges which had been granted to it. He is acting, he says, in order to restore to the Church peace and tranquillity and

> after a mature deliberation, we do, out of our certain knowledge, and the fullness of our Apostolic power, SUPPRESS AND ABOLISH THE SAID COMPANY: we deprive it of all activity whatever, of its houses, schools, colleges, hospitals, lands, and, in short, every other

1 Quoted by Jonathan Wright, "The Suppression and Restoration" in Thomas Worcester (ed.), The *Cambridge Companion to the Jesuits* (Cambridge University Press, 2008), p. 263.

2 Wright, The Suppression, p. 263.

3 For this correspondence, sec Melville, *John Carroll*, pp. 33-36.

> place whatsoever, in whatever kingdom or province they may be situated; we abrogate and annul its statutes, rules, customs, decrees, and constitutions, even though confirmed by oath, and approved by the Holy See or otherwise; in like manner we annul all and every of its privileges, indults, general or particular, the tenor whereof is, and is taken to be, as fully and as amply expressed in the present Brief as if the same were inserted word for word, in whatever clauses, form, or decree, or under whatever sanction their privileges may have been conceived. We declare all, and all kind of authority, the General, the provincials, the visitors, and other superiors of the said Society to be FOR EVER ANNULLED AND EXTINGUISHED, of what nature soever the said authority may be, as well in things spiritual as temporal.[1]

The instructions to the local ordinary were clear, though they were not always carried out to the letter. In Bruges the Jesuits were briefly confined to the Flemish college and a Dominican was put in charge of the school though many of the boys were summoned home. The - now - ex-Jesuits from Bruges either returned to England or made their way in groups, usually with a small party of their former pupils with them, to the house at Liège. About a dozen had made their way there and, by the end of 1773, twenty-three boys had joined them. Three years later there were 133 boys at Liège[2] and the school, in the same building as the College, was flourishing. The school and what became known as the seminary remained together for the next three-quarters of a century.

The community in Liège learned of the Suppression in September. The students of philosophy and theology had gone as usual in August to the villa house at Chèvremont, and they discovered what had happened only on

1 http://reformation.org/jesuit-suppression-bull.html, accessed 1 July 2013. As might be imagined, this particular source is not especially friendly towards the Society and introduces the text with the words "This Brief or Papal Bull is a damning indictment of the Papacy....The Pope acknowledges how utterly corrupt the Jesuits are, yet his suppression came AFTER their expulsion was a fait accompli by the kings of France, Portugal and Spain", the author's logic apparently being that he should have acted sooner.

2 Chadwick, *St Omers*, p. 359.

their way back when they passed a group of their professors making their way to the villa. While there was much distress and talk of leaving all in the hands of God, in the end they fared rather better than did many - or perhaps any - Jesuit communities elsewhere in the world, thanks largely to the Prince-Bishop of Liège, François Charles de Velbrück. Like many of his contemporaries in the Church, Velbrück was not in orders when selected in 1772, but was ordained to the priesthood and consecrated bishop within a fortnight, all at the age of nearly 53. He was a man of the Enlightenment,[1] eager to cultivate in his domain the sciences and the arts, and to care for the wellbeing of his subjects. He had no wish to see the disappearance from his city of a community which helped to educate his citizens, and which brought to the city a sizeable income. The members of the community were no longer Jesuits, and could not dress as such nor hold such public devotional exercises that were of Jesuit origin. Some of those not in orders returned to the status of laymen, some of the Americans, including John Carroll, made their way back home. But for the most part the community survived, and for the next few years carried on much as before. On 15th December Velbrück announced in the *Gazette de Liège* that he had himself established an English Academy, with the, now former, Jesuit John Howard as its President. He made a similar announcement in other journals elsewhere in Europe. Then, on 15th September 1778, he obtained a papal brief *Catholici Praesules* erecting the College into a Pontifical Seminary, thus permitting the President to present his students as candidates for ordination.[2]

On Howard's management of the College there were strongly held opinions. John Carroll, writing to Charles Plowden from Maryland on 10th April 1784 thought that his death, on the previous 16th October, would deal a mortal blow to the Academy. "Poor Mr. Howard!", he wrote, "what a dreadful loss to the Academy & what an unexpected stroke to me! I had long considered him not only as my friend, but as an active and zealous friend, on whom I knew I could depend, whenever I should have occasion to put his friendship

1 Chadwick says that he was "almost certainly a freemason", though he is careful to add that there had so far been no papal condemnation of freemasonry (*St Omers*, p. 364). In fact there is no evidence of his masonic membership.

2 Whitehead, *English Jesuit Education*, p. 152.

to the test ... I fear indeed, it will be fatal to the academy, when added to the stoppage of the Bavarian pension and its heavy debts".[1] Plowden himself, a future Provincial, was on the other hand rather less complimentary. As a consequence of the Suppression Howard was required to live outside the College itself, and took up lodging with the Canonesses of the Holy Sepulchre, serving zealously as their chaplain and spiritual director. Too zealously, in the view of some. As George Oliver put it in his *Collections*, "Unfortunately he was much divided between the English Nuns in that City [Liège], and his own immediate subjects, to be practically and efficiently useful, as he might otherwise have been[2]. He was replaced by a wholly different character, William Strickland[3].

William Strickland was born near Kendal in October 1731 (he died at his house in Poland Street, London, on 23rd April 1819) and entered the Society in 1748. After ordination in June 1756 he served in Liège as a lecturer in philosophy for a year (1757-58) before returning to England to work on the mission for a quarter of a century, being based mainly in Northumberland though in 1764-65 he was chaplain at Stonyhurst, then the possession of the Weld family. After the Suppression he was elected superior of the ex-Jesuits working in the North-East, and it was as the representative of the North-East of England that he attended the conference at the Turk's Head Tavern in Gerard Street, Soho from April 29th to 7th May 1776. The conference had been called to discuss how the funds of the former Jesuits would be handled. In the course of the meeting the future of the Liège academy was guaranteed, as far as possible, by the agreement of the former Jesuits resident in England to support it financially and to consider it as their seminary.

Strickland had been a leading figure in the Turk's Head conference and before Howard's death, he had visited the Academy - in what precise capacity he made the expedition to Liège is unclear - and had apparently

1 Hanley, *John Carroll Papers*, Vol. I, p. 145.

2 Op. cit., p. 104. In Plowden's view the decline, which John Carroll commented upon (see above, pp 40ff) had begun long before Howard's Presidency, cf. the quotation in Whitehead, op. cit., p. 126, footnote38.

3 Much of what follows draws upon Geoffrey Holt, *William Strickland and the Suppressed Jesuits* (London, British Province of the Society of Jesus, 1988).

persuaded Howard to mend his ways. Given his reputation in money matters - he kept meticulous records - he was an obvious choice to sort out the financial chaos which Howard had left in his wake but before accepting the Presidency of the College he circulated a questionnaire to all former Jesuits: would they accept priests educated in Liège as partners and heirs to the former Jesuit property? The responses, as far as they survive, were not encouraging but in the autumn of 1784 Strickland accepted the post nonetheless.

Two major problems faced Strickland as he took up his new office, staffing the College and financing it. There is no clear account of how he resolved the first, except that, as he informed Charles Plowden, he hoped that young ecclesiastics educated in the Academy "must undoubtedly enter into an obligation to serve the Acady [sic] at least for a limited time"[1]. Money was even more intractable an issue. The American-born Joseph Semmes was in Bavaria in 1781 trying to restore the grant that had long ago been made by the Dukes but, as a former Jesuit remarked, "Mr Semmes received the congratulation of his friends & everything except money".[2] The funds originally destined for the College in perpetuity had, it seems, been diverted to the purposes of the Knights of Malta of the Lingua (i.e., region) of Anglo-Bavarica, a new "lingua" which apparently had its eyes on funds from other religious institutions in Bavaria as well as those of the English ex-Jesuits. Strickland also tried to recover the income from the vineyards just outside Rome[3], but the Cardinal to whom responsibility had been given for the administration of the former Jesuit properties was unwilling to hand them over on the grounds - rather spurious grounds as contemporaries believed - that it was unclear how in the past the money from the wine-making had been spent. "Honest men only will be willing to do that justice [i.e., restore the Roman properties to the Liège foundation] and honest men are hard to find, sometimes even in Rome", Strickland wrote in 1801 to Marmaduke Stone who had succeeded him as President of the Academy in 1790.[4] In the end the main hope for the maintenance

1 Cf. Holt, *Strickland*, p.16. As will be seen below, this was a policy which was certainly in place later.

2 Holt, *Strickland*, p. 16.

3 See above, p. 14.

4 Holt, *Strickland*, p. 30.

of both the school and the seminary were the funds of the former Jesuits in England which, as agreed at the Turk's Head Tavern, were to contribute to the support of ten to twelve students for the priesthood. Some individual former Jesuits also left money to the Academy in their wills, occasionally a surprisingly large amount of money from individuals who had, until a fairly short time before, been vowed to poverty.

Their generosity had a purpose. Though there were some dissenting voices, support for the Academy in the eyes of the former Jesuits was in a sense a commitment not only to the education of future priests trained in the Jesuit tradition, but also a commitment to the future restoration of the Society, something which most believed would eventually happen. Whereas in England the priests were scattered in ones and twos around the country, in Liège there was a community of some forty or more maintaining as far as they could the traditional life and religious practices of the Society. By any standard the community was a large one, and financing it was a problem which, as has been seen, John Howard had failed to tackle. He had, on the other hand, considerably updated the curriculum of the school, taking his lead from the redoubtable Mother Mary Christina Dennett of the Canonesses of the Holy Sepulchre who had done much to reform the teaching in the Sepulchrine school in Liège.[1] About the year 1780 a new prospectus was drawn up for the Academy, which encompassed both the school and the seminary, almost as if the two were seen as a single unit. It says very little about the theology which is to be taught, though it included lectures on "Universal history, sacred and profane, ancient and modern", and the two years of philosophy which preceded it seem to be devoted entirely to the study of the various branches of mathematics together with "natural philosophy", topics, in other words, such as astronomy, mechanics and optics. The prospectus is in French, but it is worth translating the opening paragraphs:

1 Later at New Hall, near Chelmsford in Essex. For the development of the school, see Whitehead, *English Jesuit Education*, pp. 127-36. He believes that the education offered at Liège was in advance of almost anything that might be found in England at that time, particularly in its emphasis on science and mathematics.

Plan of Studies
At the English Academy, under the special protection
of HIS HIGHNESS, at Liège

> The fundamental aim of this Academy is 1. Religion, 2. Study, 3. Education & 4. for those destined to become ecclesiastics, every branch of Theology. Those studying at the Academy are taught English, French, German, Italian, Latin, Greek & Hebrew.
>
> In the course of the classes are taught the principles of good taste in Literature. Instruction is given in Poetry and Rhetoric. Students learn Arithmetic, Geography in detail, Algebra, the Elements of Geometry, & of Architecture; Heraldry[1], Chronology, History. Classes in Philosophy, Physics, Astronomy and Theology are preceded by six other classes.[2]

From across the Atlantic John Carroll was writing regularly to his former colleagues. In May 1783 he sent a student to the Liège Academy. In June 1785 he was requesting Strickland to seek from the bishop the ordination of one of his Marylanders, Joseph Edenshink.[3] Writing from Rock Creek on 13th November 1786 he tells Charles Plowden how glad he is to read his account of the Liège Academy but, he tells him, its apparent success won't stop him - Carroll - trying to establish something similar in the United States.[4] Not long afterwards Carroll was again writing to Plowden, seeking to recruit staff from Liège to teach at Georgetown. One of those he was trying to recruit was Plowden himself. He did so in a letter dated from Baltimore on 24 February 1793, which predicted the fate that was indeed to befall the Academy: "If the appearance of a rupture between them [the French] & that nation [England] have ended in open hostilities, the academy at Liège will meet no mercy; and

1 Many of the students came from noble - or at least arms-bearing - families.

2 The "Six other classes" are then described in detail. The French text is given in Whitehead, *English Jesuit Education*, pp. 217-20, the translation is mine.

3 The note is a formal one, in Latin, for which Hanley provides an English version, inexplicably translating "Leodiensis" as Lyons, *John Carroll Papers*, vol. I, p. 190.

4 Hanley, *John Carroll Papers*, vol. I, p. 220.

your lovely pupils will fall back again into the asylum of their Fathers immediate protection ... If the Liège Academy has met the catastrophe which I apprehend, you will not be unmindful of our deplorable want of a president for Georgetown".[1]

At the date of the letter the Academy had not met a catastrophe, though it had been a close call. In the aftermath of the start of the French Revolution there was an uprising in Liège in August 1789. The Prince-Bishop of Liège César-Constantin-François de Hoensbroeck, who had succeeded Velbrück five years earlier, was brought back from his summer residence and kept under house arrest in the city's episcopal palace. The period of citizens' rule ended on 12th January 1791 when an imperial army entered the city, freeing the Bishop who, amid much rejoicing, made a solemn entrance into his cathedral before visiting, in April, the English Academy which had been left largely untroubled by the insurgents.

On 28th November 1792, however, there came a rather greater threat to the Academy from the French revolutionary forces under the command of General Dumouriez, who entered the city after defeating the Austrian army. For a night French troops were billeted in the College, but otherwise the community escaped unscathed, both Dumouriez and his second in command General Dampierre showing themselves friendly to the English residents of the city. This may have had something to do with the fact that Dumouriez's aide-de-camp, Philip Devaux, was himself a former student of the Academy. Not that he was particularly welcomed by the community who judged him, in the words of John Laurenson, "a thorough-paced revolutionary".[2] Though

---

1 Hanley, *John Carroll Papers* vol. II, pp. 83-84.

2 Quoted by Chadwick, *St Omers*, p. 380. Fr Laurenson, who was the college's librarian, wrote an account of the events, starting at 1789. It is on his very detailed narrative that all - Chadwick, Whitehead, Opsomer - depend for the story of the migration from Liège to Stonyhurst. Laurenson, born in Essex in 1765, was a remarkable man yet has been somewhat overlooked, as perhaps librarians are wont to be. Unlike most of the Academy's community, he seems to have been prepared for the migration. Once the school was ensconced at Stonyhurst he taught mathematics there as well as, apparently, occasional classes in the humanities - he was reputed to be an excellent scholar of Latin. He translated a number of spiritual works from French and transcribed the Jesuit William Weston's own biography, published by Philip Caraman SJ in

the Academy was untouched, despite France declaring war on England at the beginning of February 1793, this was not true of the rest of the city, and it was with considerable relief that the citizens of Liège marked the retreat of the French in early March because of the advance of imperial troops.

Relief was, however, to be short-lived. Fearing the return of the French the Sepulchrine nuns made preparations to leave and did so on the night of 29th May 1794, travelling down the Meuse on coal-barges. Even the former Jesuits made some efforts to find an alternative to Liège, one of their number, a Westphalian ex-Jesuit, journeyed to what was not yet Germany in search of accommodation for the Academy, but returned unsuccessful. They had even, it would seem, been offered Stonyhurst by Thomas Weld of Lulworth Castle, a former student of the college and someone who stayed there often[1]. It was possibly during one of his visits that he made the offer of the house which he had inherited in Lancashire and scarcely used. Charles Plowden, writing from Lulworth to Lord Arundell of Wardour in August 1793, told him that Marmaduke Stone was unwilling to make the move to Stonyhurst. "The masters are advanced in age", he wrote, "& are not disposed to encounter the hardships of transmigration, and founding a new college on an extensive plan among the strong opposition which it is easy to foresee. They have a debt at Liège which if they should now pay they would have nothing left for the new establishment".[2] However large the debt may have been, the Academy's procurator set about paying it off in preparation for an urgent departure.

In May 1794 it seemed that the moment had come. The French army under General Jourdan was close by and the Prince-Bishop, the last in a long

1955 as *William Weston: The autobiography of an Elizabethan*, from a much damaged manuscript. From Stonyhurst he established a new parish, and built a church, at Clitheroe, and from 1808 until 1830 he was chaplain at Brough Hall near Richmond where he completed his account of the migration. In 1830 he returned to Stonyhurst as spiritual father to the seminarians, but two years later went to the parish at Bury St Edmunds where he died in September 1834.

1 He died at Stonyhurst in 1810, after suffering a stroke while attending a college feast. His eldest son, also Thomas, renounced his inheritance after his wife died, became a priest and, in short order, a bishop and a cardinal, the latter two, it should be said, more by accident than design. See my *The Cardinals* (Norwich, Canterbury Press, 2010), pp. 227-29.

2 Quoted by Holt, *William Strickland*, p. 25. Even Pope Pius VII, it seems, encouraged them to stay put (ibid.).

line, informed Marmaduke Stone that Liège could not be defended: he himself was soon to depart. Some of the boys from the school who lived within a reasonable distance were sent home, the remainder of the community took to the road and walked the eighteen miles to a house which had been rented across the border at Wyck, which was at the time a separate township but is now a suburb of Maastricht. They were away a week, but then - or so they believed - the situation took a turn for the better and they marched back again. But now preparations for departure began again in earnest. Barges were hired. A horse and cart was used to take goods down to the wharf. Even that was not without problems, for the retreating army tried to commandeer it and were only prevented from doing so by the intervention of another former student, now aide-de-camp of the general in charge of the imperial army, the Prince of Württemberg. The librarian packed up in chests some of the more valuable books and sent them off downriver to the house at Wyck. As he later ruefully recalled, the chests were too large and extremely difficult to manoeuvre. When they got to Maastricht there was a dispute between the handlers on the wharf and the Academy's own servants, which had to be resolved by recourse to the magistrates: happily for the librarian it was decided in favour of the Academy.

On 14th July the community set off for the barges awaiting them, already loaded, at the wharf. Unfortunately there had been little rainfall and the Meuse was running low, so low that the heavily- laden barges could not be launched into it. Some of the baggage was removed, enough to float the barges, and it was auctioned off, there and then, on the quayside and the community sailed down to Maastricht with the remainder. They arrived there in the evening and made their way, some to the house that had been rented at Wyck, some to the house which had been rented by the Sepulchrines and was now standing vacant: how many were in the group is unfortunately not recorded and cannot be calculated - nor, indeed, how many barges had conveyed them down the river.

They stayed at Wyck until 23rd July when they set sail again, destined for Rotterdam. It is not clear why they stayed so long, but it is quite clear why they suddenly had to move on: a bridge was to be thrown across the Meuse to speed the retreat of the imperial army and, had they not left when they did, they would have found their passage blocked. They again left in a rush, leaving much behind, and completely forgetting the chests of books which had been sailed down to Wyck three weeks before. It is possible that they intended to come back, certainly many continued to yearn for Liège long after they had settled at Stonyhurst. John Carroll could not understand it, neither the hasty departure nor the nostalgia. "I sincerely wish", he wrote to Charles Plowden from Baltimore on 15th April 1795, "that all at Liège had taken as timely a precaution as you[1], to secure themselves & the effects of the College. By the account, which young Matthews gave me I apprehend, that many valuable articles were left behind in Holland, which could not be carried off in time & are now assuredly and irrecoverably lost. I heard from Mr Strickland, that several members of the Liège College cannot give their minds heartily to the forming of a new establishment, & still flatter themselves with a prospect of Liège. This, I own, is inexplicable to me. Foreign colleges were resorted to, in very bad & cruel times, merely as a means for the preservation of Religion: and the necessity was always mentioned, as a very grievous oppression, which it undoubtedly was. I therefore cannot discover, on what principle any Englishman can shrink from aiding a literary establishment in his own country, who would give his assistance to one in a foreign land".[2]

The weather, at first fair, turned foul. The awnings over the barges were inadequate and they were short of food. The journey to Rotterdam, with unlooked-for interruptions, took eight days and the party only reached their destination on the 31st July, the feast day of St Ignatius, the founder of the Jesuits: they arrived too late for the priests to say mass. At Rotterdam they were met by a former lay brother, who had left the Society at its Suppression and had since become a prosperous merchant. He put up some of the party in his own house and found lodgings for the others. He also found them a ship, the *John o'Yarmouth*, under the command of a Captain Scott. It was bound for Hull and set sail on 7th August. Once again much had to be left behind which the former brother said he would look after. On 13th August the ship arrived at Harwich where some disembarked in order to visit their families, the remainder continued on to Yarmouth, where they were entertained by

1 Plowden had left Liège long before the rest of the community.

2 Hanley, *John Carroll Papers*, vol. II, p. 139.

Captain Scott's wife, and finally reached Hull. By this time there were twenty-one passengers. They included Herman Kamper, the Westphalian who had gone looking for accommodation in Germany, the American Joseph Semmes and the theologian Thomas Ellerker. In addition there were four students for the priesthood, a couple of servants from Liège who had opted to remain with the community and a dozen boys for the school. There was a delay at Hull while one of the servants was registered under the 1793 Aliens' Act[1] and then the journey began again, and once more by barge, up to Selby where they arrived on the 24th August and where they were taken to be Frenchmen and jeered at. They then continued on to Skipton by canal. From Skipton, Ellerker and Semmes hired a chaise to take them to Stonyhurst, reaching their destination on the 28th August. Others, who had taken different routes, were already there. The Academy President Marmaduke Stone and Charles Wright its procurator (his father had been a city banker) had gone from Harwich to visit the Welds at Lulworth and, after a few days there, travelled to Stonyhurst accompanied by Thomas Weld's son, also Thomas, who, as has already been remarked, was one day to become a cardinal. Stone and Wright expected to be the first to set foot in their new home, but they were not. Shortly before they arrived on 27th to take possession of Stonyhurst Fr Notley Young, a Marylander who had also disembarked at Harwich and had then travelled via London, made himself known to the resident steward. "Is this Mr Weld's chateau?" he asked.[2]

1 Whitehead, *English Jesuit Education*, p. 179.

2 Chadwick, *St Omers* p. 395. Notley Young returned to America, dying in Washington in 1810.

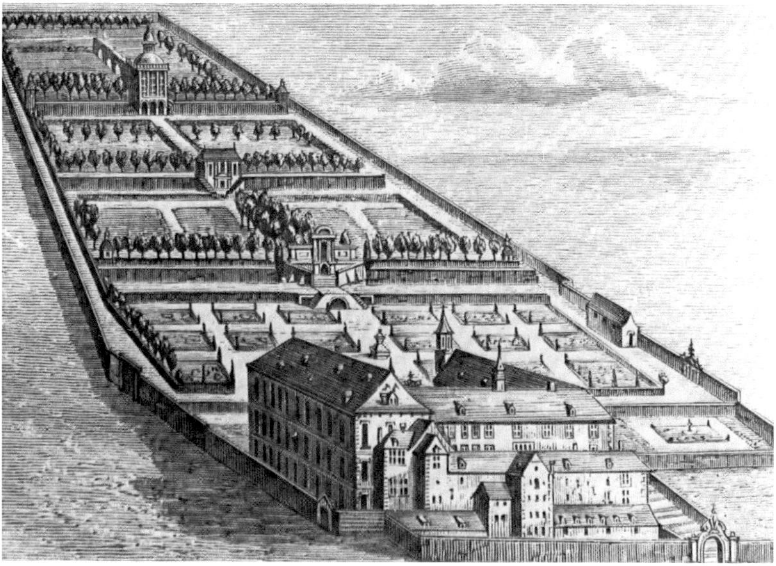

The Jesuit college in Liège, 1624-1794

Dukc Maximillian I of Bavaria (1573-1651) whose donation in 1627 helped establish the Jesuit college in Liège. The patronage of his family is commemorated in the College coat of arms

Rev John Howard SJ (1718-1783),
President of the English Academy at Liège, 1773-1783

Rev John Carroll SJ (1735-1815), who studied at Liège and was later Archbishop of Baltimore and Founder of what became Georgetown University

Rev Gerard Manley Hopkins SJ (1844-1889),
who studied philosophy at Stonyhurst
and theology at St Beuno's

Rev George Tyrell SJ (1861-1909),
who taught philosophy at Stonyhurst
and was later condemned for modernism

Stonyhurst College, Lancashire, where the English Jesuits studied philosophy from 1794-1926 and theology from 1794-1848

St. Beuno's College, Tremeirchion, North Wales, where the theology collegewas based from 1848-1926

STONYHURST 1794

The building which had now become the new home to the Academy - the establishment soon reverted to the title College - was described by Hubert Chadwick, a long-time resident: "in 1794 [it] was an unoccupied 'Hall', standing above the Ribble valley on the lower slopes of Longridge Fell which rises above to the north. The building had begun in an expensive style in 1592 by Sir Richard Shireburn on the site of an older house and was not completed: a half-house, as Oliver Cromwell described it - 'the finest half-house' he had ever seen. There had been minor additions in later years, for which Sir Nicholas Shireburn (1650-1717) in particular was responsible. But the solid columned entrance tower, designed to form the centre of the western front, still lacked a northern wing. Through a stately entrance, guarded by Sir Nicholas's wrought-iron gates, one entered an incomplete 'quadrangle', whence could be reached by a wide balustrade stairway a large and imposing banqueting hall at the far side".[1] Sir Nicholas's only heir, a daughter, died childless in 1754, and the property subsequently was inherited by Edward Weld, who was the grandson of Sir Nicholas's sister. The Welds very occasionally visited, but for the most part Stonyhurst was unoccupied after the death of Sir Nicholas, apart from a steward to look after the house and the estate, and a priest to say mass in the chapel for the local Catholic population.

The property was not simply handed over to the former Jesuits - at least, not at first. When Fathers Stone and Wright visited Lulworth after their escape from Liège, discussion presumably took place about the terms of their occupation of Stonyhurst. It was agreed that there should be a ninety-nine year lease, the first seven years at a rental of £30 a year, then at £60 a year. Three years later the terms were changed. Instead of the rent, one boy was to be educated free of charge and after seven years two boys. In 1803 Weld offered the Fathers the neighbouring Hodder Place, which had become vacant at the bankruptcy of its former tenant, with some land for £25 a year. On the feast of St Ignatius, 31st July 1809, Weld finally made over as a free gift to the English Jesuits, as they had again become, Stonyhurst with some fifty-two

1 Chadwick, *St Omers*, pp. 400-401. Chadwick unfortunately gives no reference for the Oliver Cromwell quotation.

acres and Hodder with forty-seven[1].

It was not simply the extremely generous terms which had been offered them by Weld that made Stonyhurst such an attractive proposition to the refugees from Liège. It was also its location. It was remote, in the far north of Lancashire, not easy to get to, as the journey of Ellerker and others had demonstrated. Though Jesuits had been operating in England, more or less openly, for a century or so, the Order was technically proscribed as well as, not so technically, suppressed by the Papacy. There was not much that could be done about the first, such political issues were largely in the hands of the laity, but there was hope that some way might be found to bring the Province back into existence. This hope was based upon the survival of the Society in Russia, or more precisely in that part of Poland which Russia had acquired through the partition of 1772, "White Russia" or "Alba Russia" as it was often called. The Empress Catherine had refused to allow *Dominus ac Redemptor* to be published in her dominions because she needed the Jesuits for the education of her Polish Catholic subjects. Only three years after the publication of the Brief suppressing the Society, therefore, Rome relented enough to allow the ordination of Jesuit priests in Russia. In 1780 a noviceship was opened and two years after that a General Congregation of the Society elected a Vicar General, Stanislaus Czerniewicz. Learning of this John Howard wrote to the Vicar General from Liège asking if members of his community might be allowed to affiliate themselves with the rump of the Society. Fr Czerniewicz replied that only Jesuits actually residing in Russia were to be allowed to join: American Jesuits, who made the same request, received the same answer.

And then there was the problem of the Paccanarists. After the Suppression two nascent religious orders had been formed, the Society of the Sacred Heart and shortly afterwards the Fathers of the Faith, both of which

1 Chadwick, *St Omers*, pp. 400-01. This was a remarkably generous gesture, not least because Thomas Weld had not flourished at the English Jesuit school at Bruges - the city to which the St Omer school had been forced to move after the suppression of the Society of Jesus in France - and had transferred to the French-speaking college of the Society at Pont-à-Mousson. Weld died on the Feast of St Ignatius while on a visit to Stonyhurst. See Maurice Whitehead, "In the Sincerest Intentions of Studying": The Educational Legacy of Thomas Weld (1750-1810), *Recusant History* 26 (2002-2003), pp. [illegible]

quite explicitly set out to imitate the Society of Jesus, including adopting its constitution. The founder of the second of these was the flamboyant Nicholas Paccanari, and when the two came together, as they did though with some difficulty, they became known by Paccanari's name. They hoped to recruit former Jesuits, including in England,[1] though in the end the organisation disintegrated and a good many of its members journeyed to St Petersburg to enter the Society of Jesus as part of the Russian Province. Strickland believed that forces in Rome - he mentions the Spanish - who were wholly opposed to the revival of the Jesuits were using the existence of the Paccanarists to prevent the Society's re-establishment. He was furthermore afraid that, after the 1803 union of the English Jesuits with the Russian Province, the General would ask him to take over the loss-making College set up by the Paccanarists in London's Kensington, together with its considerable debts - as indeed the General did. Rather than the former Jesuits joining the Paccanarists, after 1803 there was talk of some of the Paccanarists joining the English Jesuit community: "I know the prejudice of some of our Gentlemen against foreigners & therefore will not attempt to urge any opinion of mine", Strickland wrote to Stone in 1804, "but I own that it appears to me a desirable thing for the College to have a native of every country in Europe amongst your teachers and directors".[2] What Stone thought of this suggestion is not recorded, but he had problems enough without trying to integrate into his Stonyhurst community priests from a different tradition, albeit one that mimicked the Society. The school was one thing that might be expected in the long term to look after itself provided enough teachers could be found, the seminary presented rather greater problems. Stone, who had something of a reputation as a ditherer, acted uncharacteristically promptly in petitioning Rome for the recognition of Stonyhurst's status as a pontifical college to train men for the priesthood, the status that had been granted to Liège by the brief *Catholici Praesules* of 1778. On the application of the Congregation of Propaganda, under whose oversight as a missionary country England fell, this was renewed in favour of Stonyhurst at a papal audience in February 1796. The Seminary could now present candidates for ordination.

1 They apparently recruited one former English Province Jesuit.

2 Holt, *William Strickland*, p. 46.

But for ordination you needed a bishop. In 1790 William Gibson had succeeded his older brother[1] as Vicar Apostolic - effectively Bishop - of the Northern District within which Stonyhurst lay. The brief had guaranteed Stonyhurst's own independence as a Seminary: the issue remained, what was to become of priests after they had been ordained? And the answer to that question could not be resolved until another one had been answered: were the "Gentlemen" of Stonyhurst members of a religious order, or were they "secular" clergy (they could hardly be called diocesan priests because until the restoration of the hierarchy in 1850 no dioceses existed in England and Wales). If they were the former, then their placement after receiving holy orders was determined by their religious superior; if the latter, then they were at the disposition of the local Vicar Apostolic, and the disposal, in other words, of "the bluff lack of cordiality"[2] of Bishop Gibson. In 1802 Rome granted a rescript to Stonyhurst "which confirmed the wording of the oath that had long been taken at Liège and Stonyhurst before ordination; the students were to promise that after eight years of teaching at Stonyhurst (if required) and the reception of orders when it seemed good to the president, they would do missionary work in England or Wales permanently under the Vicars Apostolic".[3]

This gave rise to a further consideration. Jesuits in England had established many missions, or parishes, around the country and carefully husbanded their resources to support them. They had continued to supply many of these missions even after the Suppression of the Society and wanted to go on doing so from Stonyhurst but if they were at the disposition of the Vicar Apostolic then this could not be guaranteed. Indeed, the whole ownership of the property of the former Jesuits was in question. A rescript of the Congregation of Propaganda dated 15th July 1786 said that although property formerly in the hands of the Society could continue to support former Jesuits for as long as they lived, they had no right to dispose of it and, at their deaths, it was to become the property of the mission under the control of the Vicars Apostolic. Strickland believed that this rescript was issued at the request

1 And wanted his younger brother to succeed himself!

2 David Matthew, *Catholicism in England, 1535-1935* (London, Longmans, 1936), p. 171

3 Holt, *Strickland*, p. p. 55..

of Bishop Matthew Gibson of the Northern District, whereas his predecessor, and Bishop Challoner in the London District, had said they would not attempt to exercise authority over it. Strickland believed this to be the attitude of most of the Vicars Apostolic at the time. Responding to the Rescript Strickland cited *Praemunire*, the fourteenth-century Acts forbidding appeal from England to Rome, though it is not altogether obvious that they applied. In any case, Gibson did not pursue the matter. But some method had to be found to preserve the Jesuit "inheritance". The approved means was for one priest to will his property to his successor. This was a very unsatisfactory arrangement, open to all sorts of confusion, and Strickland wanted to set up a trust to handle all the funds of the former Province, at least in part as a means of holding the (ex) Province together. This was not accepted, though some of the individual districts followed his advice for themselves. It would all be a great deal simpler were the Society to be reconstituted in England.

It was therefore imperative that the status of the Gentlemen of Stonyhurst as members of a religious order be acknowledged as soon as possible. In the end that took a very long time to achieve. The first step in the process had to be the re-establishment of the English Province. As has been seen, despite the language of *Dominus ac Redemptor* which declared the Society of Jesus to be "for ever annulled and extinguished"[1] the English former Jesuits had always maintained the hope that the 1773 Brief would not prove to be as definitive as its author clearly intended. And they had good reason for their optimism: the restoration seemed likely enough. Not only had the Society survived in Russia, as has been remarked, but in 1793 the Duke of Parma asked for the Society to be reconstituted in his duchy and Pius VI gave verbal consent. The papal brief *Catholicae Fidei* of March 1801 confirmed the existence of the Society in Russia and in Parma, and in 1804 it was formally restored in the Kingdom of Naples and Sicily. Meanwhile, however, Cardinal Ercole Consalvi, the papal Secretary of State, had written in a letter of 2nd July 1802 that the Russian Jesuits could after all accept former Jesuits from outside the country. This was communicated to Gabriel Gruber, the rector of the Jesuit house in St Petersburg in October, who then wrote to Strickland

1 See above, p. 43f.

asking the names of those who wished to join the White Russian province and "in May 1803 the English ex-Jesuits received the Pope's permission to do so".[1] Strickland began writing round to all the former members of the Society, inviting them to re-join it. Thirty-one did so although at the time there were seventy-three surviving from the old province. There were various reasons why some did not re-enter, including age, but an important reason why some failed to rejoin was the fact that there was nothing in writing. The Pope had given verbal permission for the affiliation of the English ex-Jesuits to the General's agent in Rome but felt unable to make a more public pronouncement because of the continuing hostility of the Spanish government. And even though he gave verbal permission he added a rider that those joining the White Russian province should not wear Jesuit dress.

Now the English Province of the Society of Jesus had been re-established with the verbal approval of Pope Pius VII there was need for a provincial. In his correspondence with the General in Russia, Strickland had urged the merits of Marmaduke Stone, and his opinion prevailed: a letter dated 1st March 1803 appointed Stone as English Provincial, with authority over Ireland and Scotland as well.

The English Jesuits were, however, in an anomalous position. Privately they were Jesuits by what they took to be the Pope's verbal assent; publicly they were still secular clergy. Everything therefore now depended on the attitude of the Vicars Apostolic. It was not long before their stance was known. They collectively petitioned Rome. A letter dated 3rd December 1803 from Cardinal Stefano Borgia, Prefect of the Congregation for the Propagation of the Faith ("Propaganda" as it was, and still is, generally known) instructed the bishops "not to recognize those who wished to be Jesuits in England, nor to admit their privileges, supposing they claim any, unless the Vicars Apostolic are first certified of the legitimate existence [of the Society], and this by the authority of the Holy See through the Congregation de Propaganda Fide".[2] Borgia, who was no sympathiser of the Jesuits, though he had attempted to preserve their work on the foreign missions, wrote again on 17th March 1804 insisting there had been

1 Holt, *William Strickland*, p. 56.
2 Holt, *William Strickland*, p. 63.

verbal approval (*vivae vocis oracula* was the phrase used) of the union between the Russian Jesuits and those outside Russia.

This made little difference. The English Jesuits now had a Provincial and had built a noviceship at Hodder Place, but the arguments about the validity of their aggregation to the Jesuits in Russia dragged on. Stone suggested that anyone offering themselves to the Society should study philosophy before taking vows, in the hope that the situation would become clearer. The General, now Thaddaeus Brzozowski, in 1807 wrote to Strickland about a letter of 1802 in which an Italian theologian reported Pius VII's words in response to a petition on behalf of the English Jesuits by some of the English Catholic gentry. The Pope had spoken in Italian, but it was reported in Latin: *"Procedatur sane, sed in habitu seculari ut olim fiebat; hocque pro praesenti sufficit"* ("Let them go ahead, but in lay dress as they used to, and that will do for the moment")[1].

All this may have been encouraging, but it wasn't exactly definitive. While little better could realistically be expected from a Pope who was having to cope with the Society's enemies in Rome as well as with the unpredictable Emperor Napoleon. Propaganda issued a decree in August 1813 while Pius VII was a prisoner of Napoleon's at Fontainebleau which in effect abolished the privileges which had been carried over to Stonyhurst from Liège but then, on Christmas Eve that same year Pius VII - still at the time incarcerated at Fontainebleau - issued the necessary rescript, confirming the verbal approval a decade earlier for the English (ex) Jesuits to become part of the White Russian province. Priests could now be ordained *titulo paupertatis*, at least in theory. In practice it was not quite so straightforward. It left the English Jesuits in something of a no-man's land. This was especially so when it came to dealing with the Vicars Apostolic in England and the bishops in Ireland. Priests are ordained to a "title", that is to say before ordination they must show they have a means of earning their keep. Priests to be are therefore ordained for a specific diocese which will support them or, if they have enough money, on their own patrimony. Those who are members of a religious order, on the other hand, are ordained *titulo paupertatis*, to the title of poverty, which means in effect that the order will look after them. But the Jesuits did not formally

1 Holt, *William Strickland*, p. 71.

exist in Britain and Ireland until they had the approval of the Vicars Apostolic, and if those who had studied for the priesthood in the seminary[1] at Stonyhurst were ordained *titulo missionis*, for the mission, they were, strictly speaking at the beck and call of the hierarchy after they had served eight years at the College as required by their oath. As has been mentioned, the Jesuits had long had their own places of apostolic activity in England, and the newly ordained might hope to be sent to these, but unless their status as religious was clear, the whereabouts of their service would be determined by the Vicars Apostolic. Even after the Bull *Sollicitudo Omnium Ecclesiarum* of 7th August 1814 by which Pius VII formally brought the Society of Jesus back into being, some of the Vicars Apostolic continued to refuse to acknowledge the existence of the Society within the region under their jurisdiction.

The problem arose at least in part because of the general issue of Catholic emancipation, the regaining for the Catholics of the British Isles of the full rights of citizenship. A group of laymen, with the support of the majority of the Vicars Apostolic, were prepared to take an oath which, according to the most obvious interpretation, would have implied that Catholics accepted, indeed approved of, toleration for all religions. This was not official Catholic teaching until the Second Vatican Council,[2] and the English Jesuits and others were not prepared to sign up to it. The most notable opponent was the sturdy friend of the Gentlemen of Stonyhurst, Bishop John Milner, Vicar Apostolic of the Midland District. He was "a dominant and vigorous character, who refused any kind of concession to the civil government. His attitudes were dominated by opposition to government interference and to lay usurpation of clerical authority. He resisted proposals for a government veto over Catholic episcopal appointments and became much involved in Irish affairs, acting as agent for the Irish Catholic bishops in London. Urged on by the Irish bishops

---

1 When the community first moved to Stonyhurst, all inhabited the same building. In 1803 the novitiate opened at Hodder Place but the scholastics stayed where they were until 1830 when the "seminary" was built - later to be called St Mary's Hall (see below, p. 87). It was extended in the 1880s. It was the home of Rome's English College, the Venerabile, from 1940 to 1946. See Geoffrey Holt, "The Seminary", LLNN 96 (2004), pp. 354-57.

2 For a brief history of official Catholic attitudes to religious freedom see my article in the festschrift for John Wilkins' "Religious Freedom: The Limits of Progress" in *Unfinished Journey*, edited by Austen Ivereigh (London, Continuum, 2003), pp. 134-148.

he resisted the willingness of his fellow Vicars Apostolic to exchange the right of veto in return for Catholic emancipation, believing that it would compromise the independence of the Church. On this issue, not for the first time, Milner stood almost alone against the prevailing mood of English Catholic opinion. Thus a bill for Catholic emancipation on those terms was lost in 1813 and political liberty for Catholics was not achieved until after Milner's death, but the veto plan was abandoned".[1] The theological stance of members of the Society, in other words, was regarded by many as inimical to the wider needs of the Church in Britain and Ireland. With the exception of Bishop Milner of the Midland District the Vicars Apostolic refused to ordain Jesuits *titulo paupertatis* despite both the 1813 rescript and the papal Brief of 1814 on the grounds that the latter, unlike the Brief of Suppression, had not been formally communicated to them through the proper Roman channels, in other words, by the Congregation of Propaganda. Despite intense lobbying by the English Province neither the Pope, nor the Prefect of Propaganda, was prepared to bring pressure to bear on the bishops in England. Those in Ireland had readily accepted the return of the Jesuits. "The conduct of your Vicars is inexplicable to me", the Dominican Archbishop John Thomas Troy of Dublin[2] wrote to Bishop Milner in November 1818. In Ireland, he went on, Jesuits "are ordained *titulo paupertatis*, and in every respect constituted according to the rules of the Society. Not a murmur of opposition to them from our clergy, or from Protestants or government".[3] The opposition of the Vicars Apostolic to the Society was, however, endorsed by the Papal Secretary of State, the nonetheless Anglophile Cardinal Ercole Consalvi,[4] when he wrote to Bishop William Poynter, Vicar Apostolic of the London District, that the Society could

1 Judith F. Champ, "Milner, John (1752-1826)", *Oxford Dictionary of National Biography* (Oxford University Press, 2004); online edn, Jan 2008 [http://www.oxforddnb.com/view /article/18791, accessed 26 Aug 2013].

2 Troy had for many years served as prior of the Dominican basilica in Rome, San Clemente, which may perhaps in part account for his strongly pro-Roman convictions.

3 Quoted by Edwards, *Jesuits in England*, p. 167. For a more detailed, though rather quaint, account of this controversy, see Edwards, *Jesuits in England*, pp. 159-72.

4 For a brief account of Consalvi see Michael Walsh, *The Cardinals* (Norwich, The Canterbury Press, 2010), pp. 179-184. He achieved the remarkable feat of extracting from King George III a Hanoverian pension for Henry Cardinal Duke of York, the last significant Stuart pretender to the English throne.

not be considered reconstituted in England unless the civil authority had done so which, he must have known, would have been a highly unlikely turn of events.

These issues were crucial for the future of the Seminary - indeed of the whole Stonyhurst enterprise, school as well as seminary, given that the alumni of the latter were expected to serve, if required, for eight years in the former to maintain the teaching staff. But if those offering themselves to the Society, and a novitiate had been opened at Hodder Place in 1803 in anticipation of new vocations, with Charles Plowden as novice master, could not be guaranteed ordination, then there was no point in anyone joining. There was much to-ing and fro-ing with Rome, the Papacy and Propaganda apparently at odds over the status of the English Jesuits. In 1820 Poynter received the letter from Consalvi just referred to. "Never did the prospects of the Society in England seem bleaker", remarks Francis Edwards,[1] and some of the candidates for ordination just gave up and went home.

And there was another problem, threatening the whole enterprise. In 1813 the (Protestant) Irish patriot Henry Grattan had introduced into the Westminster parliament[2] a Catholic relief act which would have allowed Catholics access to all but the highest offices of state. It seemed to be going through until the Speaker put forward a motion to ban Catholics from sitting in Parliament. The bill therefore failed. The argument about Catholic relief had turned upon the right of the government to veto episcopal appointments in the Catholic Church, which many of the laity were prepared to live with, as indeed were some of the clergy, though certainly not Bishop Milner. There was much acrimonious debate both within the Church and in the public arena about the loyalty to the Crown of the Catholic hierarchy. As it happened, the same debate was taking place in Canada, where it appeared to turn even nastier and threatened the Church's control of its schools. It was in this context that the Marylander Fr Nicholas Sewall, at the time on the staff at Stonyhurst,[3] wrote on 15th February 1815 from Liverpool to an unnamed correspondent

---

1 Edwards, *Jesuits in England*, p. 168.

2 After the Act of Union of 1800 Ireland was governed from Westminster: Grattan sat as the member for Dublin City.

3 And later Provincial, in succession to Charles Plowden.

but presumably the Provincial Marmaduke Stone: "From repeated articles in newspapers it appears evident that a storm is gathering and will soon burst on Stonyhurst & the whole English Province. Some time ago you & I had some conversation on the Canadian affairs & you said, very justly, that it was time for us to look about & to secure our Property in case Government should adopt any such measures as were ordered in Canada. You then, I think, proposed to reconvey the Property to Mr Weld, who in case of need could swear that it was his & this I think exceedingly proper & necessary to be done, as soon as possible".[1]

Happily this never became necessary, but the hostility of the Vicars Apostolic continued unabated. As a consequence in 1820 the General Congregation of the Society, called to elect a new Jesuit Superior General, decreed that English candidates for the Society should study in Rome where at least they could be ordained *titulo paupertatis*. Charles Plowden, who had been chosen as Provincial in 1817, went to Rome for the Congregation, but afterwards stayed there for some time once more to attempt to persuade the Pope to force the English bishops to respect the constitution *Sollicitudo*. He failed, and on 13th June 1821 died suddenly at Jougne in France during his journey home. He was buried there, with full military honours, under the misapprehension he was a soldier: he had, after all, been attending the election of a General.

The consequences of the General Congregation's decision are apparent in the Province catalogues[2] for the period. The catalogues show a steady stream of novices from 1803 onwards, but only a handful made the transition from the noviceship to the Seminary to study philosophy and theology. There they were taught by a very small and undistinguished[3] group of professors with

1 ABSI Letters of Fr Stone, Fr Sewall and Fr Connell, folio 18. The Mr Weld mentioned is the Thomas Weld who had first accompanied Frs. Stone and Wright to Stonyhurst. At this point in 1815 his wife was still alive and it was not until three years after her death that he decided to become a priest, though not a Jesuit.

2 The catalogues, copies of which were sent to the Jesuit headquarters in Rome, list the members of a province and in which community they were living.

3 An exception should perhaps be made for Fr Norbert Korsack (1773-1846), Polish by birth, who entered the Russian Province c. 1787. In 1805 he was sent by the General with two others to reopen the mission in China, and the group was expected to come to London to purchase

no special training in the disciplines they were required to impart to the scholastics. Not all the catalogues survive, if they ever existed, but whereas that for 1820 records three people studying theology and ten philosophy, the 1823 catalogue, after the 1820 decision of the General Congregation, records six studying theology in Italy and three likewise in Italy studying philosophy. There were three more theological students in Switzerland. Even the novices had moved: they were now in France. The English bishops had succeeded where the Suppression of the Society and the French revolutionary armies had failed: they had shut the English Jesuit seminary.[1] Well, not entirely. The seminary did not quite shut; there remained a small staff at Stonyhurst, including Norbert Korsack, and it was back in operation by 1828 though with very few students.

The date of 1828 is surprising, because the situation with the Vicars Apostolic had not changed. They were still refusing to recognise the Society and ordain its candidates *titulo paupertatis*. When the change came, it did so quite suddenly, through the intervention of Bishop Augustine Baines, a Benedictine and coadjutor bishop of the Western District, who was sympathetic to the Society's predicament and, in 1828-1829, was in Rome for health reasons. He was highly thought of by the Pope of the time, Leo XII[2], and when he sent Leo a note about the situation in England he received it back on 29th January 1829 with a note in Leo's own hand declaring that the constitution *Sollicitudo*, which in 1814 had restored the Society throughout the world, did indeed have canonical force in Britain. This, at last, was something the Vicars Apostolic could not ignore. But when, later that same year 1829, the most important of the Catholic Relief Acts was passed by Parliament, it was evident

astronomical instruments - he and the other priest with him, who eventually found his way to America, were mathematicians and physicists. Korsack was taken ill, went to Stonyhurst to recover, and never left. The catalogues record he taught dogmatic and moral theology and also that he served as missioner in nearby Clitheroe.

1 "The students of philosophy and theology live outside the province", notes the catalogue for 1825, when there were twelve students of the latter but only five of the former. A further remark about the novices indicates that the noviceship was suspended for six years ("sex annorum interjectu interruptam"), during which time they were sent to other provinces. It adds that they were re-integrated on 21st September 1827.

2 Leo wanted to make him a cardinal but Baines refused the offer.

that the bishops' fear that recognition of the Society might delay Catholic Emancipation had indeed some foundation. It was not strictly speaking Jesuits alone who were denied the right to exist in England, all religious orders of men were banned by the Act. Only the Jesuits, however, were mentioned by name:

> "And be it further Enacted, That if any Roman Catholic Ecclesiastic, or any member of any of the orders, communities or societies hereinafter mentioned, shall, after the commencement of this Act, exercise any of the rites or ceremonies of the Roman Catholic religion, or wear the habits of his order, save within the usual places of worship of the Roman Catholic religion, or in private houses; such ecclesiastic or other person shall, being thereof convicted by due course of law, forfeit for every such offence the sum of Fifty pounds.
>
> And whereas Jesuits and members of other religious orders, communities or societies, of the church of Rome, bound by monastic or religious vows, are resident within the United Kingdom; and it is expedient to make provision for the gradual suppression and final prohibition of the same therein; Be it therefore Enacted, That every Jesuit, and every member of any other religious order, community or society of the church of Rome, bound by monastic or religious vows, who at the time of the commencement of this Act shall be within the United Kingdom, shall within Six calendar months after the commencement of this Act, deliver to the clerk of the peace of the county or place where such person shall reside, or his deputy, a notice or statement, in the form and containing the particulars set forth in the Schedule to this Act annexed; which notice or statement, such clerk of the peace, or his deputy, is hereby required to preserve and register amongst the other records of such county or place, for which no fee shall be payable, and a copy of which said notice or statement shall be by such clerk of the peace, or his deputy, forthwith transmitted to the chief secretary of the Lord Lieutenant, or other Chief Governor or Governors of Ireland, if such person shall reside in Ireland, or if in Great Britain, to one

of His Majesty's principal Secretaries of State; and in case any person shall offend in the premises, he shall forfeit and pay to His Majesty, for every calendar month during which he shall remain in the United Kingdom without having delivered such notice or statement as is hereinbefore required, the sum of Fifty pounds.

And be it further Enacted, That in case any Jesuit, or member of any such religious order, community or society as aforesaid, shall after the commencement of this Act, within any part of the United Kingdom, admit any person to become a regular Ecclesiastic or brother or member of any such religious order, community or society, or be aiding or consenting thereto, or shall administer or cause to be administered, or be aiding or assisting in the administering or taking any oath, vow or engagement, purporting or intended to bind the person taking the same to the rules, ordinances or ceremonies of such religious order, community or society, every person offending in the premises in England or Ireland, shall be deemed guilty of a Misdemeanor, and in Scotland shall be punished by fine and imprisonment.

And be it further Enacted, That in case any person shall after the commencement of this Act, within any part of this United Kingdom, be admitted or become a Jesuit or brother or member of any other such religious order, community or society as aforesaid, such person shall be deemed and taken to be guilty of a Misdemeanor, and being thereof lawfully convicted, shall be sentenced and ordered to be banished from the United Kingdom for the term of his natural life".[1]

This draconian legislation against religious orders seems from the start to have been a dead letter. It was, however, considered wise to take precautions. As far as the Jesuits were concerned the ban on wearing a religious habit was unimportant because, at this date, they did not wear one, but when they took

1 Roman Catholic Relief Act (10 George IV, c. 7), 13th April 1829. The text, accessed 28th October 2013, can be found at http://multitext.ucc.ie/d/The_Emancipation_Bill

vows the ceremony took place privately rather than publicly, with just the novice candidate for the Society and a priest being present, a custom that survived until the 1870s.

The enforced exile and exposure to continental customs and methods of study brought some changes to the Stonyhurst Seminary. The staff was slightly increased and the catalogues record the professors as teaching more specific disciplines. In 1831, for example, Norbert Korsack was teaching not just theology but dogmatic and moral theology and Scripture, while Vincent Jaffré taught logic, metaphysics and ethics. One can only presume that hitherto Scripture had been taught though there is no mention of it as a particular discipline distinct from theology. It would have been odd if it had not previously been taught at all. Certainly, as has been seen, Hebrew was part of the curriculum at Liège and Edward Slaughter, a professor at Liège who, at the beginning of the eighteenth century served a term as the College's rector, had published a Hebrew Grammar in 1699 which was still in print nearly two centuries later.[1] In 1800 Strickland gave Stone advice on remedying the shortage of lecturers by allowing the student clergy to study the languages of the Bible, Hebrew and other oriental languages, on their own. He had been much exercised by the loss of books from the library during the flight from Liège, and wrote to Stone with ideas about how they might be recovered. In the meantime he had acquired for the seminary library "a small pamphlet on the Hebrew language. It is in high estimation with the learned in these parts & at Oxford. I think you would do well to encourage the study of that & other oriental languages. A house like yours shou'd not be without two or three men versed in them", he wrote.[2]

Among the specialisms which began to appear in the catalogue, starting in 1832, though the office itself must have been considerably older, was that of "teaching philosophy to externs". It had been the custom at Liège, as has been seen, to teach a small group of laymen alongside the Jesuit

1 He also published a book on mathematics, cf. p. 26fn4. The Hebrew grammar first appeared in Amsterdam in 1699, there was another edition at Rome, 1705, and five subsequent editions at Rome (1830, 1834 - this was published by the Collegio Urbano of the Congregation for the Propagation of the Faith - 1851 - a revised edition - and 1861), with a final edition at Paris in 1867.

2 Holt, *William Strickland*, p. 32.

"philosophers" - though, it must be remembered, philosophy had then a wider connotation and included mathematics and some science. This practice continued at Stonyhurst, with the lay philosophers living in some style in the seminary. The problem for Catholics was that the Test Acts effectively banned them from Oxford and Cambridge. At Cambridge these tests were applied at the end of the course, just before taking a degree - which made it possible for Catholics to matriculate at Cambridge and study there, though not to graduate - whereas at Oxford they had to be taken on matriculation which meant Catholics could not attend at all. The same problem did not apply in Scotland nor in Ireland and Catholics had been attending Trinity College Dublin from 1793. Stonyhurst had been preparing boys to go to Trinity as well as to attend Scottish universities. To remedy the lack of higher education for Catholics, Bishop Baines, the Vicar Apostolic of the Western District, had been eager to start his own university and had purchased Prior Park for this purpose, but the university had failed to get off the ground though its associated school continued to flourish.

The need for a separate institution became less pressing when the University of London was established in 1835. It was simply an examining and degree-awarding body which at the time consisted of two already existing colleges, University College and King's, and it was possible for Catholic institutions to apply for affiliation - which Stonyhurst did, along with several others. This brought an element of discipline to what seems to have been a somewhat easy-going existence on the part of the so-called "Philosophers" - hunting, shooting and fishing, with the very occasional lecture or expedition to the library. At least for those who opted to study a degree, that louche life-style came to an end.[1] "I do not believe any of the boys from the sixth forms of our public schools are better prepared [for their degree]", commented one University examiner in 1867. "I do not think it possible that they could have a better education given to them than Stonyhurst gives".[2] That was very

1 The course for the lay philosophers has been studied in detail by Vincent Allen McClelland in *English Roman Catholics and Higher Education, 1830-1903* (Oxford, Clarendon Press, 1973), upon which these paragraphs very largely depend. Cf. pp. 28-45, a chapter dedicated to Stonyhurst.

2 Quoted, McClelland, *English Roman Catholics*, p. 36.

flattering, no doubt, but McClelland points to the deficiencies of the education that was received. The proud scientific tradition of at least the latter years at the Liège Academy did not survive despite the establishment of an observatory in the grounds of the College in 1838-39. The College simply did not have the resources to venture far beyond the traditional Jesuit fields and even there success was questionable. As one Rector of Stonyhurst remarked in 1872, "We do not come near Eton, Rugby, Cheltenham, Wellington ... in scholarship (Greek verse is utterly unknown to us)".[1]

This English experiment in Jesuit higher education for laymen came to an end in 1916 when the Military Service Act introduced conscription and made the status of lay philosophers impossible to maintain. Indeed, no candidates had been presented for London Honours Degrees since 1891 and in 1895 the ban on Catholics attending the universities of Oxford and Cambridge was lifted,[2] thus making attendance at the two ancient English universities a very attractive alternative to a London-based degree studied in the remotest part of Lancashire. When Catholics were at last allowed to attend Oxford and Cambridge the Jesuits promptly[3] opened a house at Oxford, now Campion Hall, intended only, however, for the education of members of the Society.[4]

While it is possible to work out what the lay philosophers were studying,[5] it is much more difficult to discover what the Jesuit scholastics were being taught in what was at that time only a two-year course: the changeover to a three-year one came in 1860 on the instructions of the then

1 McClelland, *English Roman Catholics*, p. 32. McClelland's interpretation of this report by Fr Purbrick is vigorously rebutted by Henry Sire in his *Gentlemen Philosophers* (Worthing, Churchman Publishing, 1988), pp. 42-43, a work which I came across only after this book was completed.

2 The religious tests had been removed in 1871: that Catholics were forbidden to attend ether Oxford or Cambridge was a decision of Rome, at the request of the English bishops who were spurred on by the Archbishop of Westminster, Henry Edward Manning. Manning himself, a convert to Catholicism, was an Oxford graduate and one-time Fellow of Merton College.

3 In 1896.

4 English Jesuits had of course long obtained degrees elsewhere. In the catalogue for 1843 there is the first mention of Jesuits, four of them, studying for a University of London degree, no doubt alongside the lay philosophers. The entry does not recur, but the practice continued.

5 The Heythrop Library has a collection of Honours papers.

General of the Society, Peter Beckx. He also laid down in his letter of 1858 that the philosophy taught, and of course the theology, should be that of Thomas Aquinas. The question is, what were the scholastics learning up to this time. In his examination of the early years of the poet Gerard Manley Hopkins,[1] Alfred Thomas quotes a letter of 1846 about the parlous state of seminary education from John Henry Newman, then in Rome, to his friend, and eventually fellow Oratorian, John Dobrée Dalgairns.

> Hope told me we would find very little theology here, and a talk we had yesterday with one of the Jesuit fathers here shows we shall find little philosophy. It arose from our talking of the Greek studies of the Propaganda[2] and asking whether the youths learned Aristotle. 'O no - he said - Aristotle is in no favor here - no, not in Rome - not St Thomas. I have read Aristotle and St Thos, and owe a great deal to them, but they are out of favor here and throughout Italy. St Thomas is a great saint - people don't dare to speak against him - they profess to reverence him, but put him aside.' I asked what philosophy they *did* adopt. He said *none*. 'Odds and ends - whatever seems to them best - like St Clement's Stromata. They have no philosophy. *Facts* are the great things, and nothing else. Exegesis but not doctrine.' He went on to say that many privately were sorry for this, many Jesuits, he said; but no one dared oppose the fashion[3].

Whether the views of the Jesuit to whom Newman was talking should be taken entirely at face value may perhaps be doubted. Whatever had been the situation earlier, by 1846 Giuseppe Pecci, a Jesuit and cardinal-to-be (and brother of

---

1 Alfred Thomas *Hopkins the Jesuit: The years of training* (London, Oxford University Press, 1969).

2 Newman is writing from the college attached to the Congregation for the Propagation of the Faith - Propaganda for short - which had oversight over Britain as it was, at the time, a missionary country.

3 Quoted, Thomas, *Hopkins*, p. 94. The whole letter, which for the most part discusses the state of theology and the fact that Newman had heard that "Theologians of the Roman College, who are said to sway the theology of Rome are introducing *bits* (without having seen the whole book) *bits* of my Essay into their lectures to dissent from", is three pages long. Cf. John Henry Newman, *Letters and Diaries* vol. XI (London, Nelson, 1961), pp. 279-282.

the future Pope Leo XIII) was professor of the critical history of philosophy at the Jesuit university in Rome, the Gregorian. He was a leading advocate of the study of the philosophy and theology of St Thomas, and was to become a major figure in the preparation of his brother's 1879 encyclical *Aeterni Patris* which urged on the Catholic Church the study of the philosophy of St Thomas. But this is towards the end of the nineteenth century. It is more difficult to discover what scholastics were being taught in the early years of that century. Thomas quotes Frederick Copleston: "In the seventeenth, eighteenth and early part of the nineteenth centuries philosophy in ecclesiastical seminaries and teaching institutions tended to take the form of an uninspired Scholastic Aristotelianism amalgamated with ideas taken from other currents of thought, notably Cartesianism and, later, the philosophy of Wolff".[1] Christian Wolff (1679-1754), Copleston adds elsewhere, by writing "separate treatises on ontology, cosmology, psychology, natural theology, etc."[2] was largely responsible for the division of philosophy into the separate disciplines that may be seen allotted to different lecturers in the catalogues from the early 1830s onward. As has been remarked, it may be no accident that the greater specialisation in philosophy follows closely upon the enforced sojourn of the scholastics on the continent, thanks to the intransigence of the Vicars Apostolic. It has to be remembered that the teaching, and the textbooks, were all in Latin whether on the continent or in England, so the transference of, say, Roman methods and structures, was not a problem. On the other hand there is no evidence that any of the lecturers had received any further philosophical or theological education beyond that which they had themselves received in the seminary. If they did, they must for the most part have been self-taught, and as, in the first half century at Stonyhurst, they did not leave behind them any published treatises or, for that matter, any unpublished ones either, we have no clue to exactly what they taught.

The picture becomes somewhat clearer after the publication of *Aeterni Patris,* though only marginally so. In his autobiography Fr George Tyrrell, later to be condemned as a Modernist and denied a Roman Catholic burial,

1 *History of Philosophy* vii (London, Burns and Oates, 1963), pp. 387-88, quoted Thomas, Hopkins, p. 93.

2 *History of Philosophy* iii (London, Burns and Oates, 1953), p. 356

describes how he arrived at Stonyhurst to study philosophy shortly after the publication of the encyclical:

> Father M., with the tendency of most geniuses to embrace unpopular causes, had taken it [the encyclical] up loyally, and was preaching "Aquinas his own interpreter," as opposed to Aquinas filtered through the brain of Suarez. For many years previously the study of the long-forgotten text of Aquinas had led Father Liberatore and other Italian Jesuits to see that Suarez had missed wholly some of the subtler and all-pervading principles of the great doctor, that he had conceived in a gross and imaginary form the distinctions of a purely intellectual character, and had thereby materialised the entire system. Now though the ancient Jesuit constitutions insisted on Aquinas as our theologian and philosopher *par excellence*, in the course of time, for obvious reasons, Suarez had become a household god, and the anti-Dominican animus had thrust St. Thomas into the background, except as diluted and tempered in the pages of the Society's own doctors. Hence the Liberatore school was whispered against as disloyal to our traditions. But the present Pope [Leo XIII] had come under its influence, and when the *Aeterni Patris* came out, it was a blow in the teeth of the main body of the S.J. - a triumph for our enemies and the traitors in our own camp.[1]

The "Father M." mentioned by Tyrrell is almost certainly Father Thomas Rigby who at the time was teaching logic and metaphysics.[2] Rigby was, however, in a minority among the lecturers in espousing unadulterated Aquinas. As Tyrrell indicates, the Jesuit tradition had been to understand Thomas through the writings of Francisco Suarez (1548-1617), regarded in his own day as a leading philosopher and theologian though he is today remembered,

1 *Autobiography of George Tyrrell*, edited by M. D. Petre (London, Edward Arnold, 1912), vol. I, pp. 242-43. It has to be remembered that Tyrrell, who came to reject scholasticism, by the time he wrote his autobiography was not exactly a neutral observer.

2 Cf. David Schultenover, *George Tyrrell: In search of Catholicism* (Shepherdstown, The Patmos Press, 1981), pp. 25 and 364.

if at all, as one of the earliest theoreticians of international law. In his theological writings he associated himself with the theories of his fellow Jesuit Luis de Molina (1535-1600), whose writings on grace and free will contradicted the theories of the Dominican Domingo Bañez (1528-1604). The controversy about the relationship between grace and free will dragged on for twenty years, with innumerable inconclusive debates taking place in the presence of the successive popes until in 1607 Pope Paul V forbade any further argument. He did, however, allow the opposing parties each to teach their own theory as long as they did not describe their opponents' views as heretical.[1] It was out of this debate that there arose the "animus" mentioned by Tyrrell to explain the tenacious clinging on, despite the papal ukase, to the interpretation of Aquinas through Suarezian eyes by members of the teaching staff at the Stonyhurst seminary.

There was much debate. "Father T.", Tyrrell remarks, "the prefect and controller of studies, not only tolerated but rather enjoyed all this ferment, which, as contrasted with the sleepy lethargy of former years, seemed a symptom of a waking mental activity".[2] But there was only so much dissension the Stonyhurst community could tolerate. In 1884 Thomas Rigby was sent out to the Demerara mission, to what is now Guyana, ostensibly because - apparently much to the consternation of the other lecturers - he thought the programme of studies in the Seminary could be improved, but really, or so Tyrrell believed, because he had been critical of the Suarezians among the staff.[3]

1 It is known as the "de auxiliis" controversy.

2 Tyrrell, Autobiography, p. 246. "Fr T." is not easy to identify, but Schultenover suggests it was Joseph Rickaby (1845-1932), a friend of Tyrrell's and a considerable author. He was also the translator of *The Practice of Perfection and Christian Virtues* by Alphonsus Rodriguez SJ, a little of which Jesuit novices had read to them each day. In its earlier guise, a translation published in two volumes by the English College Press at St Omer at the end of the seventeenth century, it was used widely by English religious of many congregations, male and female, and its influence deserves to be studied. Unlike the original translation, Rickaby's version could be highly entertaining. The two brothers, Joseph and John Rickaby, were the children of the butler to William Constable-Maxwell, who afterwards acceded to the revived title of Baron Herries in the peerage of Scotland. Constable-Maxwell paid for them to go to school at Stonyhurst when his own son was sent there.

3 Cf., Schultenover, George Tyrrell, p. 31. The Thomas v. Suarez debate was more significant in philosophy than it was in theology. Among those lecturing in philosophy Suarezianism only

If little can be discovered about what was being taught in the first half of the nineteenth century, more is known about the structure of a student's day. He rose early, at 5.30 am, and breakfasted at 7.30 am. In between there was a meditation and mass. There were two lectures in the morning, at 10.00 and 11.15, then dinner [sic] at 1.00 pm. After dinner there was recreation until 2.30 pm, then a "Circle", to be explained shortly, for an hour at 3.15. Three hours were then devoted to study, followed by supper, more prayer, and bed. On Sundays, Tuesdays and Thursdays the period of recreation after dinner was prolonged until 5.30 pm and once a month, on a Thursday, there was a "Blandyke", a whole day without study. On such days the students - scholastics - would be allowed out on "long walks" in threes, not necessarily with companions of one's choice. It was of course a religious community as well as a house of study, and the year was punctuated with liturgical feasts, which were celebrated in the refectory as well as in the chapel. On such occasions there was often wine and a "postea", a drink after dinner. These were also the few times when the various communities in the house might mix. During the first half of the nineteenth century there were four different communities living in the Seminary: there were the lecturers, mainly priests, though some teaching was done by able scholastics; there were those studying theology; there were those studying philosophy; and there was a small group of lay brothers, Jesuits who had no wish to become priests and who provided most of the housekeeping. For the most part the distinct communities expected to keep to themselves, but on feast days the two groups of students were allowed to mingle.

The same thing happened year after year. The philosophy course was at first two years, but a directive from the Jesuit General, Peter Beckx, which insisted that the teaching of St Thomas be the staple diet within the Society, extended it to three from 1861. The timetable may have varied slightly, but the round of feasts according to the Roman calendar never varied. The sacristan kept a log book: so many candles and of which kind on the altar on any given feast, which vestments would be worn, and so on. Likewise the senior student,

gradually died out: there was still a Suarezian teaching epistemology at Heythrop in the early 1960s. It survived even an irritated instruction to the Society by Pope Leo XIII in December 1892, ordering it to obey the spirit, rather than find ways around the letter, of *Aeterni Patris*. The new papal missive made little difference.

known as the Beadle, kept a detailed log, recording comings and goings, but also what happened in the classes, and when. "Circles" were part of this process, a teaching device which was a throw-back to the Middle Ages and yet was still in use, at least in philosophy, well into the second half of the twentieth century. The technique all turns upon the syllogism, something the scholastics would have learnt at the very beginning of their course of study. There are many types of syllogism, but only the most basic is really relevant. In its best-known form it runs:

All men are mortal
Socrates is a man
Therefore Socrates is mortal

In a medieval disputation the defendant proposes the thesis, or the major premise ("All men are mortal"), then introduces the particular case, or minor premise ("Socrates is a man"), and then draws out the inevitable, or what he hopes is the inevitable, conclusion: "Therefore Socrates is mortal". In a "Circle" someone objected (the objicient, usually there were two of them) and tried to prove the thesis invalid. He did so by attempting to show that the major proposition might be understood in a number of different ways and, while it might be true in one sense, it was not necessarily true in the other senses, with the result that the conclusion could not logically be drawn from the premises as stated. Of course, the major premises were usually much more complex than the one quoted here for illustration,[1] but it had to be presumed that the major premise was, at least in some sense, true: it was regarded as the height of bad form to deny flatly the truth of the major premise ("Nego majorem", the objicient would say, for all these disputations took place in Latin). It was just about acceptable to deny the minor, but more commonly the minor was subjected to minute examination in order to distinguish the various meanings which could be attributed to it: "Ad minorem, distinguo ..." The defendant

1 For instance, the indefatigable Fr Alfred Thomas identified a number of theses which might have been defended by Gerard Manley Hopkins. To take just a couple of examples, Lex [naturalis] est immutabilis, universalis, aeterna et legis positivae fundamentum: "The [natural] law is unchanging, universal, eternal and the foundation of positive law" or Philosophus neque tenetur neque potest omnia demonstrare vel definire: "A philosopher should not be required to, nor can, demonstrate and define everything". Cf., Thomas, *Hopkins*, p. 122.

would then respond by examining the objicient's distinctions.[1] Towards the end of the session there was an opportunity for the rest of the class, who supposedly had of course been listening, to bring their own objections to the thesis proposed by the defendant.

These exercises in logic-chopping usually took place twice a week, and occasionally there would be rather grander occasions in the presence of the rector and other worthies of the community in which the brighter students were selected to perform so as to demonstrate their prowess. It now seems all very arcane - though the BBC's Third Programme in the 1960s thought it worthwhile to broadcast some of these conducted in English by the Dominicans of Oxford - but this was an essential aspect of the seminary's method of teaching. In a class a thesis was proposed by the lecturer, he then ran through the objections to this thesis raised by other philosophers, both medieval and modern, he answered the objections to his own satisfaction and thereby proved his thesis. But it was not only a teaching method, it was also means of examining a student's capabilities. During the end-of-year examinations a candidate would be faced with a selection of theses which he had been taught in that year and was required to defend them in the approved manner, against the objections put by one of the panel of three examiners. All of this was, of course, taking place orally and, as has been said, in Latin. The results, in effect marked out of ten, were also given in Latin: a perfect ten was "summa cum laude" while a nine was still "magna cum laude" and so on, terms still sometimes used in continental universities. These examinations were typically half an hour per course, and a student would have done several courses during an academic year. At the end of three years there was an examination "de universa philosophia", on the whole of philosophy, in which a scholastic would have to defend for an hour, and still in Latin, a selection of theses drawn from any of the courses he had studied while in philosophy. Arcane though it now may seem, this structure of teaching and examining, though in later years not always in Latin, survived down to the 1960s.

1 "The great Jesuit theologian Vasquez declared that he had entered religion convinced by a syllogistic argument he had heard Bannez [sic] the Dominican give in his lectures, but that, once he was a Jesuit, he had found a flaw in the syllogism", Joseph Crehan, *Father Thurston* (London, Sheed and Ward, 1952), p. 25.

As has already been remarked, there was a reasonable amount of time for recreational activities for the students. In this regard Stonyhurst's very remoteness was an advantage, for there was a good deal of open country round about in which to go walking. Moreover the River Hodder ran nearby, with fishing and swimming for those so inclined. In the summer there were cricket matches, in the winter there was skating. There was also a "villa", a fortnight's holiday, as a community, away from the seminary itself. In 1865 a house had been purchased as a holiday home for Jesuit scholastics in Barmouth, North Wales, though this, it seems, was at first intended mainly for the theologians who by that date had left Stonyhurst, also for North Wales[1]. As a philosopher in the 1870s, the Jesuit poet Gerard Manley Hopkins went with the community to Douglas in the Isle of Man, but there was no fixed location for these times away.

There were more intellectual activities. In 1870 an "English Academy" was started, which later became known as the "Phil and Lit" society and lasted for nearly a century. Students in philosophy were encouraged to produce essays on various topics - historical themes seem to have been the most popular - and then read them to each other. Some of these essays eventually found their way into *Blandyke Papers*, the - at that time - handwritten occasional magazine which the philosophers were encouraged to produce as an exercise to prepare for writing articles for publication, especially in the Jesuits' own journal, *The Month*.[2] Similarly they were also required to preach in preparation for their future ministry. This practice was known for some reason as "tones", and the sermons were subjected to the criticism of their fellow students, as well as to that of one of the priests appointed to preside over this exercise. Occasionally

1 This was Aber House, in the centre of the town. It was sold in 1879 and a house in Fronoleu Terrace, just outside the town, was purchased in its stead. In a letter to the editor of LLNN (100 [2010], p. 72), Ken Vance SJ suggests that the coming of the railway to Barmouth was considered to be something of a distraction for the young men - or, presumably, the crowds of holiday makers were the distraction.

2 It had been founded in 1864 by the remarkable convert to Catholicism Frances Margaret Taylor (1832-1900), who in 1865 sold it to the English Province, its first Jesuit editor being the prolific Henry James Coleridge. *The Month* ceased publication in 2001. Frances Taylor, who had nursed with Florence Nightingale at Scutari, went on to found the Poor Servants of the Mother of God, taking the name Mother Magdalen of the Sacred Heart.

individuals were expected to preach in the refectory, making themselves heard over the noise of their colleagues' eating. Meals were, of course, as in most religious houses, usually taken in silence while someone read: a chapter of Alphonsus Rodriguez' *Practice of Perfection and Christian Virtue*[1], a book of general interest, or during Advent and Lent of spiritual nourishment, and in Latin the "Martyrology", the list of saints whose feasts fell on that day. Refectory reading was also subjected to criticism by a priest appointed for the purpose, not so much as a preparation for reading in church (the liturgy was still in Latin), as to iron out unacceptable accents. It was, day to day, a life almost as unchanging as the natural law. Any break in the regularity was therefore usually greeted with enthusiasm, especially if they were to do with food - though there was consternation when the traditional oyster supper had to be cancelled because of the price of oysters: the beadle, the senior student, noted plaintively in his log that the molluscs had to be replaced with "Lobsters, etc".[2] And, once a month, there was the luxury of a bath.

Whatever the living conditions, academically, the situation was improving. From the 1860s there was an increase in the number of professors at the Stonyhurst seminary and the subjects taught were more clearly defined. Among the teachers was the eminent astronomer Father Stephen Perry - an observatory had been built in the college grounds, in the manner of Liège - who was elected a Fellow of the Royal Society in 1874, a very rare honour indeed for a Catholic priest.[3] He was a much-travelled scholar but also an outstanding lecturer to the students who continued in their philosophy course to study a good deal of science, especially mathematics. Perry had received

1 This is a seminal text of Jesuit spirituality, based on "exhortations" given to Jesuit communities in Spain by Alphonsus Rodriguez (1526-1616). It was first published in Spanish in 1609 and was translated in part into English as early as 1612.

2 Quoted Thomas, *Hopkins*, p. 117.

3 The *Oxford Dictionary of National Biography* describes Perry's life as "exceptionally adventurous". He was born in London in 1833 and despite being educated by the Benedictines joined the Society of Jesus in 1853. He was not only an FRS but also served on its committee. He died on board ship off the Salut Islands, French Guiana, in 1889 while observing a solar eclipse: he had caught dysentery, which developed into gangrene, from prisoners in the nearby penal settlement of Devil's Island.

considerable grounding in his chosen field, though that could not be said for many of his fellow lecturers at the seminary who seem sometimes to have taught wholly different courses from one year to the next, even in some instances a philosophy course this year, a theology one the next.

Unrest in Europe, especially in Italy in the period leading to that country's unification, brought many Jesuits, both students and teachers, to the safety of England, mainly Italians but including a number of Irish scholastics who had been studying in Rome. In 1860, for instance, Joseph Bayma arrived from the Turin province to teach metaphysics and a couple of years later he was joined by Antoninus Benincasa from Sicily and in 1871 by Nunciatus Capaldi from Naples who lectured on ethics. Later there were also Germans in considerable numbers. One refugee from Bismarck's *Kulturkampf* was Bernard Boedder,[1] who again lectured both in theology and philosophy. His more significant contribution, however, was a volume on philosophical arguments for, and about, God.[2] It first appeared in 1891 but was reprinted as late as 1927, though by then there was another similar book in the same "Stonyhurst Philosophical Series" and one with the same title - *Natural Theology* - by George Hayward Joyce who had also written an excellent, if massive (600+ pages with a learned appendix of canonical texts in Latin and Greek), historical, legal and theological study of marriage, another example of the confusing cross-over of lecturers from philosophy to theology. In the same Stonyhurst series there were books on moral philosophy, on what would now be called epistemology, psychology and logic, the last also by G. H. Joyce. Included in this list was also a work on *Political Economy* by Charles Stanton Devas, a layman who had never taught at Stonyhurst. In the earlier part of the twentieth century Devas's book was much used in schools to teach Catholic social thought.

These works were of course deeply rooted in scholasticism or rather in Neo-Scholasticism, medieval thought's nineteenth-century reincarnation.

1 The catalogue entry in the year 1900 awards him his umlaut: Bödder in place of Boedder.

2 This book was also published in Latin by Herder of Freiburg "in usum scholarum", for the use of scholars - almost certainly meaning Jesuit scholastics. It has the same structure as the English version, but follows the rigorous thesis and distinction method described above. The Longman edition is much more readable and not simply because it is in the vernacular.

Contemporary philosophers were regularly referred to, however, and not always as "adversarii", opponents to be demolished. The versatile Joseph Rickaby, who wrote a small work under the title *Scholasticism*, defending the method, in 1906 also produced *Free Will and Four English Philosophers*. The four were Hobbes, Locke, Hume and J. S. Mill, not exactly contemporary, but they were discussed and, one must assume, taught to the students in the seminary. The difficulty for the students, however, was that should they wish to study the "adversarii" further they would need permission: most of the works of such authors were firmly on the *Index of Forbidden Books*[1].

1 Though the "Index" has now been abolished, it was still theoretically in vigour until the late 1960s. Books that were listed therein were marked in the Philosophers' Library by a large white letter "L" on the spine.

ST BEUNO'S, 1848

As has just been remarked, the books mentioned appeared in the Stonyhurst Philosophical Series: G. H. Joyce's study of marriage did not. There had been a parting of the ways between philosophers and theologians. An increasing number of novices meant an increasing number of students. In 1844 the General of the Society was advised of the overcrowding in the Seminary, and insisted that there should be a separate establishment for those studying theology. The issue was so pressing that in 1845 the theologians were sent off to study abroad, though only for a year. The house in the grounds of Stonyhurst still continued to be called "the Seminary" until 1885, a term usually reserved for a college for the study of theology, but the catalogue for that year records that it was now called St Mary's Hall. At the same time the number of staff was increased - though nine out of the sixteen were listed as "cur. val.", priests looking after their health, and two more were studying not philosophy but astronomy. Because the theologians and their professors had left for Wales there was now space for a larger community of priests.

The division between philosophers and theologians had in fact come thirty years before. In 1846 the Provincial of the day, Randal Lythgoe, was making a visitation in North Wales and was going on to visit a farm which had, it seems, long belonged to the Jesuits. As Paul Edwards records, "It was on this journey that he breasted Cwm Hill, saw our valley, and, according to legend, thumped his knee and made his celebrated declaration of intent: "here I will build my theologate".[1]

Each year Jesuit superiors are expected to write to Rome to report on the state of their communities, and the work that had been done. These "Annual Letters" are a major source of information, and in the collection of Annual Letters from 1846 to 1852 there is the following account of St Beuno's:

This college was begun by Reverend Father Randal Lythgoe, the

1 Paul Edwards, *Canutes's Tower* (Leominster, Gracewing, 1990), p. 20. Another, rather more cynical, version has it that he uttered the words at the spot his horse dropped dead. For Lythgoe, see Maurice Whitehead, "Education and Correct Conduct: Randal Lythgoe and the work of the Society of Jesus in early Victorian England and Wales" in Sheridan Gilley (ed.), *Victorian Churches and Churchmen: Essays Presented to Vincent Alan McClelland* (Woodbridge, The Boydell Press for the Catholic Record Society, 2005), pp. 75-93.

> Provincial, and was completed and opened under the governance of Father William Cobb, on the feast of St Alphonsus Rodriguez [30th October] in the year 1848. It was established for the theological education of our students, and begun under particularly favourable circumstances, namely with the very well-known theologians Father Giovanni Perrone and Giuseppe Marzio, at the time exiled from Rome. It is located in a most delightful valley in North Wales, amid an ignorant Calvinist population, one blinded by prejudice and given over to superstition.[1]

The writer went on to say that the community hoped to bring the said population to the true religion and in the Annual Letter for 1855-56 remarked that the scholastics were teaching some thirty local children - not an easy matter because first they had to teach them English. "They come willingly to mass and to exhortations", he went on, "and finally submit themselves to the faith. In this way five or six are each year added to the Church". One child had converted to Catholicism without the knowledge of his parents, and refused to recant despite all blandishments.[2]

The tone of this account suggests that the Jesuits had moved into hostile territory. In fact they appear to have been made very welcome, with regular invitations from the local gentry to take part in otter hunts, invitations which they eagerly took up. The theologians were, in their turn, equally hospitable. For Queen Victoria's Golden Jubilee in 1887 they put on a dinner, largely at the expense of the College, for seven hundred villagers, followed by fireworks. This was repeated for the Diamond Jubilee and again in 1911 for the coronation of George V, though on this last occasion the Minister [Bursar], while setting off his homemade fireworks, lost his left hand in an explosion.[3]

---

1 British Province Archives (ABSI) Mss 2, U1/10/1; my translation of the Latin.

2 ABSI U1/10/2.

3 Edwards, *Canute's Tower*, p. 104. Much of the information about life at St Beuno's comes from "Seventy-Five Years At St. Beuno's: A Farewell Retrospect". This was a paper read to the St Beuno's Essay Society in 1923, though it was not quite a farewell because the move to Heythrop did not take place for another three years. The paper was written by Thomas Roberts, who makes a remark about Alban Goodier receiving the tonsure - the initiation into the status of a cleric -

In the same document recounting the origins of St Beuno's there is a lament that "The College has sustained a considerable loss through the elevation of Fr Joachim Forn to the chair of theology at the Roman College". In his place there had been appointed Fr William Cardwell who had himself completed his own theology course at the College only a couple of years before: he was later to serve as Rector. As had happened in philosophy, theology was struggling to find adequately educated professors, certainly in the nineteenth century. And again, as in philosophy, the lack was made good by the influx of scholars from abroad. There were students as well as professors from all over Italy and, after the onset of the Kulturkampf, from Germany as well. Indeed, there were so many from Germany that Ditton Hall, near Widnes, a gift to the English Province by the Marchioness Stapleton-Bretherton in 1873, was made over to them. Seventy-four arrived, of whom forty-seven were students of theology: the numbers grew to a peak of 109 in 1887.[1] Bernard Bœdder was among the students who first arrived, and there were some distinguished theologians among the exiles, not least Franz Xavier Wernz SJ (1842-1914) who taught canon law at St Beuno's 1881-82, and then later at the Gregorian University in Rome, of which he became Rector. In 1906 he was elected the 25th General of the Society.[2]

and adds of this event that Goodier was "little thinking of the pallium". Nor, clearly was Roberts, who also received the pallium, the stole worn only by metropolitan archbishops. Cf. LLNN XXIX (1924), pp. 19-33. The reference to Goodier is on p. 31. Roberts's information was largely drawn from Beadles' logs.

1 LLNN 28 (1905-06), pp. 191-92. In 1895 they moved to Valkenberg in Holland and shortly afterwards the property was sold to the Sisters of Nazareth.

2 After the implementation of the anticlerical Waldeck-Rousseau legislation in France at the beginning of the twentieth century, French Jesuits opened a philosophate in Jersey - in the Imperial Hotel, which was lying abandoned - and a theologate at Ore Place, Hastings, but individual French Jesuits do not appear to have played as much a part in English Jesuit life as did their German and Italian confreres. The theologate of the Lyon Province was evacuated to Mold, a dozen miles or so from St Beuno's, where the refugees were accommodated in a prison, the professors in the governor's house, the students in the cell block. It had been designed so that a single warder could observe all the eighty-five cell doors. As the anonymous report (LLNN XIV, p. 106) puts it, "Although the house was quite ready for use, still at all times there is a sufficient difference between a prison and a College of the Society to afford many inconveniences and trials". When they left the house, the French Jesuits sold it to an order of nuns, who in turn sold it to the Castile Province of the Society, and they to the Leon Province who, when they discovered the Jesuits were not after all to be expelled from Spain, asked the English Procurator to sell it on.

Accounts of the community at Ditton Hall emphasise its contribution to the people in the surrounding area through the work of the German priests in the local parishes and of the students in teaching catechism. The same was true of the individual Jesuits, German or Italian, who taught at St Beuno's. They even readily embraced the combative style of the English Jesuits of that era, as exemplified, for instance, by Thomas Harper. Harper was "Professor of Philosophy at the Seminary, Stonyhurst College, later Professor of Theology at the College of St. Beuno's, N. Wales". That was how the title-page of the first version of *Peace through the Truth; or, Essays on Subjects connected with Dr. Pusey's Eirenicon*, published in 1864, described him. He was himself anything but eirenic. The dedication ran "To Our Holy Father, S. Ignatius, who has been thrice assailed in the person of his children by the author of the *Eirenicon*, this volume is humbly and affectionately dedicated as an act of reparation". He was rather more explicit in the second edition of 1874: "Everyone who has read it [the first edition] must be well aware that I was forced to point out, over and over again, the absence in Dr. Pusey of those qualifications which are absolutely indispensable for anyone who takes upon himself the grave questions of theology".[1] Not that the combative Harper limited his attack to non-Catholics. In a series of articles in *The Month* he was highly critical of one of John Henry Newman's major works, *An Essay in Aid of a Grammar of Assent*. His objection, expanded upon over nearly 200 pages, was "the seeming dissidence" which he observed between the future Cardinal's position and 'what is commonly taught at present in our Catholic schools' - by which he meant scholasticism.[2]

The professors from abroad readily embraced the same polemical approach. In the 1860s, for instance, Paul Bottalla from the Sicilian Province was teaching sometimes theology, sometimes church history at St Beuno's.

1 The learned Dr Edward Bouverie Pusey (1800-1882) was of course a friend of John Henry Newman, a leading figure in the Oxford Movement and, later, the foremost ecumenist of his day, facts which do not appear to have fazed the splenetic Fr Harper.

2 Thomas Harper, *Difficulties touching certain philosophical theories propounded in Dr. Newman's Grammar of Assent*, p. 55. This book was printed for private circulation and bears no publisher's imprint, though its location, Roehampton, suggest that it was printed at Manresa, where the Jesuits ran a press. It is also undated; the articles which it reprints from *The Month* appeared in 1870.

He had not been long in the country before he published *The Papacy and Schism: Strictures* on *Mr Ffoulkes' Letter to Archbishop Manning*.[1] He quoted the said Mr Ffoulkes on the first page, adding "Assertions like this are frequent in books and periodicals written in the interests of Protestantism; they prove nothing except the ignorance of history which still prevails among certain classes". He produced two more volumes, the first in 1868 and the second two years later[2] - Part I "The Supreme Authority of the Pope" and Part II "The Infallibility of the Pope". The general title for both volumes was *The Pope and the Church Considered in their Mutual relations with reference to the Errors of the High Church Party in England*, the last phrase being printed in a Gothic typeface so there was no mistaking its import.

These were all fairly massive tomes. But then, the professors and students alike had time on their hands. In the quotation from Newman cited earlier he had commented that Jesuits choose "the most prosaic neighbourhood, if it be but populous".[3] He cannot have been thinking of the English houses of Jesuit formation. St Beuno's was almost as remote as Stonyhurst. Tremeirchion was, and remains, a beautiful location, but there is no denying it was remote and, despite the building of new roads, to some extent still is, at a distance from populous neighbourhoods. The nearest town - it only formally became a city in 2012, despite being in possession of a cathedral - is St Asaph, which is tiny: it is four and a half miles away. There is a large town and from 1848, a railway station, at Rhyl on the coast but that is eight and a half miles distance. In the nineteenth century the staff and students at the College had for the most part to make their way everywhere on foot, so the opening of a railway line in 1858 which passed through St Asaph was particularly welcome. It was also some eight miles from Holywell, a shrine to St Winefride, supposedly the cousin of St Beuno, with a sacred spring - the town still describes itself as the "Lourdes of Wales" - where the Jesuits had purchased a property in 1669.[4]

1 London, Burns and Oates, 1869, priced at 2/6d.

2 Both under the Burns and Oates imprint.

3 Cf. above, p. 6 fn1.

4 Edwards, *Canutes' Tower*, p. 23. According to legend the spring had appeared at the spot where Winefride's head bounced after she had been decapitated by a jealous suitor. Beuno reattached her head, and she went on to live a full and holy life. The shrine was a popular place of pilgrimage in the middle ages.

Gerard Manley Hopkins arrived there at the end of August 1874 and described the College, built to the Gothic design of the eminent Catholic architect Joseph Aloysius Hansom,[1] in a letter to his father:

> The house stands on a steep hillside, it commands the long-drawn valley of the Clwyd to the sea, a vast prospect, and opposite is Snowdon and its range, just now it being bright visible but coming and going with the weather. The air seems to me very fresh and wholesome ... It is built of limestone, decent outside, skimpin within, Gothic, like Lancing College done worse. The staircases, galleries, and bopeeps[2] are inexpressible: it takes a fortnight to learn them. Pipes of affliction convey lukewarm water of affliction to some of the rooms, others more fortunate have fires. The garden is all heights, terraces, Excelsiors, misty mountain tops, seats up trees called Crows' Nests, flights of steps seemingly up to heaven lines with burning aspiration upon aspiration of scarlet geraniums: it is very pretty and airy but it gives you the impression that if you took a step farther you would find yourself on Plenlimmon, Conway Castle, or Salisbury Craig.[3]

It was also extremely draughty, as Hopkins discovered to his cost.

In this remote vastness - for as Hopkins hints it was a very large building[4]- the students and staff had to make their own entertainment. On the model of the philosophers' "Phil. and Lit. Society" there was a debating club. The diligent Fr Thomas has studied the topics put forward for discussion and they do indeed, as he remarks, throw light on the ethos of the scholastic community:

> The subjects ranged over a varied selection of topics, including religion, politics, education, sociology, and ethics. Among motions debated and carried were "That Catholics should support the movement

1 He of "Hansom cab" fame, though apparently the cab that plied London's streets differed markedly from Hansom's original design.

2 Apparently unexpected hiding places.

3 Quoted, Thomas, *Hopkins*, pp. 150-51. The quotations is from Hopkins's *Journals and Papers* (London, Oxford University Press, 1959), p. 257.

4 Though with only one bath until in 1909 two more were added.

> for the disestablishment of the Church of England", "That it is desirable as far as possible to substitute day-schools for boarding schools", that "Women should be withheld from voting in elections for Parliament", "That it is a subject for congratulation that the Queen has assumed the title of Empress of India", "That the parochial clergy should interest themselves in the establishment of clubs and clubhouses for the use of the Catholic working classes", and that "The present movement for closing public houses on Sunday does not deserve our support". On the other hand they rejected these motions, "That Catholics should as far as possible abstain from controversy on religious subjects", that "In the present state of the Church a schoolmaster is more profitable to souls than a preacher", that "Catholic education has suffered from the connections of our Colleges with the London University" and that "'An Edinburgh Sabbath' is less objectionable than a 'Paris Sunday'".

Thomas notes that Hopkins himself proposed the motions, among others, that "Eminence in arms is a better object of national ambition than eminence in commerce" and "That the state does well in compelling parents to educate their children". Both were defeated. On the other hand the following, also proposed by Hopkins, was carried: "A theological student should eschew all literature not bearing on his studies".[1]

As for the studies themselves, they were described by Fr Richard F. Clarke SJ in an article entitled "The training of a Jesuit", published in *The Nineteenth Century* in 1896.[2] For the first two years there were two lectures in the morning, on moral and dogmatic theology, and two in the afternoon on either canon law or history, and dogmatic theology. There was also half an hour of Hebrew. In the third year Scripture replaced moral theology and Hebrew was dropped. As in philosophy there were circles, but "these disputations are as a rule fiercer and more searching than in the philosophical course. There often arises, not the *odium theologicum*, but the eager advocacy with which

1 Thomas, Hopkins, p. 159 (slightly adapted).

2 Vol. XL (July-December 1896), pp. 211-225. The section cited is on pp. 223-24.

even Jesuits defend their own opinions". The course was four years long, the fourth year being given over, says Clarke, largely to preparing for the final examination, which would determine one's status within the Society. The less able, however, were required only to undertake three years of theology, the "short course" for which a separate professor was assigned.[1] There were also assigned two different professors, clearly demarcated in the catalogue, one teaching dogmatic theology in the morning, one in the afternoon. Ordination followed at the end of the third year. This meant that the students had to pass an examination "ad audiendas confessiones", for hearing confessions, known simply as "ad auds". Clarke, writing as he was for a secular readership, did not mention this part of a Jesuit's training, but it loomed large, particularly as Jesuits took pride in their knowledge of moral theology - it always played a greater role in theology in the Jesuit tradition than it did in most other contexts. There would also, therefore, have been regular "cases of conscience", when problems which might be encountered in the confessional were discussed at length. Some of these "cases" were of such complexity not to say absurdity that they came to be known as "Spanish cases". There were books full of them, such as that by Thomas Slater, mentioned below, though unlike Slater's they were for the most part in Latin.

The standard of teaching could not have been very high. As has been seen, William Cardwell was summoned back to St Beuno's - in 1868 he was teaching moral theology - only two years after he had completed his own theology. Franz Xavier Wernz was given just a year of private study before he was required to lecture in canon law. Similarly John Morris (1826-1893), a convert to Catholicism and a diocesan priest before he became a Jesuit, in 1868 was sent to Louvain for a year to prepare for teaching canon law at St Beuno's, though he began his brief tenure with Church history which was rather more to his taste. "This will be a first experience for me", he wrote of

1 The "short course" lasted until Heythrop moved to London, but from 1913 it was no shorter, just academically less demanding. In the catalogues those doing the Long Course are listed as "Auditores theologiae", and those on the Short Course "Auditores theologiae moralis", though in 1873 that was changed to "Auditores Cursus Moralis et Theologiae Abbreviatae". In 1886 "Longs" was renamed "Auditores theologiae scholasticae", cf. Edwards, *Canute's Tower*, pp. 56 and 58.

the possibility of his lecturing, "as I have never taught anything in my life".[1] At Louvain he received a doctorate "which is a requisite for profession in the Society", wrote his biographer:[2] a doctorate in 1869 was clearly rather different from one a century later. In his biography there is an account of his style of teaching which one must presume was not typical of most classes at St Beuno's: "He read his lectures for half an hour in the evening in English. He would not allow us to take notes during them, so you had simply to give yourself up to listen, and a very pleasant half hour it was, an interval of sunshine in a day, otherwise neither stormy or gloomy, but certainly trying, the school-day, namely, of the theologian"[3].

Preparation for lecturing among the professors at St Beuno's was decidedly patchy. John Morris may have had a doctorate, but few others achieved - or were even given the opportunity to attempt - a higher degree. Herbert Lucas was an outstanding student of the classics, which he demonstrated by achieving first place in classics and second in philosophy when he took an MA degree at London University. He was then sent to Rome to study scripture which he taught at St Beuno's from 1889 to 1901. He wrote numerous articles, but the only serious academic topic he addressed appears to have been the life of the Dominican friar Girolamo Savanarola, hanged then burnt as a heretic in Florence in 1498. Thomas Slater was sent to Rome after ordination to take courses in both canon law and ecclesiastical history - but when he returned to the theologate he was put to teaching moral theology. Like Lucas he was a prolific producer of articles, but many of them were on his new-found discipline. He also published *Cases of Conscience for English-Speaking Countries* solved by Rev. Thomas Slater and a much reprinted *Manual of Moral Theology for English-Speaking Countries* in two volumes, which ran to several editions in quick succession. Even better known as a moral theologian was Henry Davis, despite the fact that he had absolutely no special formation. Again a notable writer of articles, mainly, though not always, on contemporary

---

1 John Hungerford Pollen, *The Life and Letters of Father John Morris SJ* (London, Burns and Oates, 1896), p. 174.

2 Pollen, *John Morris*, p. 174

3 Pollen, *John Morris*, p. 177.

moral issues, his magnum opus was his four-volume *Moral and Pastoral Theology*, a standard work in its time. But that came out first in 1935, after the move to Heythrop.

Another professor who moved to Heythrop in 1926 was Alexander Keogh. He had studied church history for two years at Innsbruck. He taught history from 1909, then from 1912 added canon law. He served as Rector from 1915 to 1922. His particular interest appears to have been early Christianity in Rome but he wrote little. Sylvester Hunter had written textbooks on the Law of Property - despite the fact that his first degree was in mathematics - before his conversion. As a Jesuit theology lecturer he wrote little, apart from a three-volume *Outlines of Dogmatic Theology*, the first part of which was published in 1895 and was reprinted in 1909, long after his death. Charles Townsend became Professor of Scripture in 1906. He was reputed to be brilliant, competent in eleven languages, but none of this can be confirmed because he apparently never put pen to paper, not even in an article for *The Month*.

One of the better teachers, though again without any special training for the post, was John Rickaby, who lectured in dogma. He

> stressed the historical element and showed how rigid, *a priori* formulae needed to be modified when that factor was taken into account. He made his pupils aware that their textbooks did not have the infallibility that their tone seemed to claim, that there was a good deal to be said against the theses that were stated so authoritatively, and he often seemed to cast doubt on whether certainty were possible at all when all aspects of the matter had been weighed. He was playful, unsystematic and eclectic. Fr O'Fallon-Pope who succeeded him was the opposite pole, utterly rigid, undeviatingly Scholastic in his opinions and wholly uninterested in other views and approaches[1].

It was just such rigidity that caused George Tyrrell, though sometime after he had left St Beuno's, to write a complaint to Camillo Mazzella, a Jesuit cardinal and the principal author of Leo XIII's encyclical, commending the

1 Edwards, *Canute's Tower*, p. 76. Both Rickaby and O'Fallon Pope were Suarezians rather than Thomists.

theology of St Thomas. Mazzella communicated the letter to the Pope and replied to the young priest that Leo had expressed the hope that Tyrrell's views would eventually prevail. News of the letter reached the Jesuit General Luis Martín, who tartly remarked that Tyrrell believed he knew more of Thomas Aquinas than all the rest of the Society.[1]

As the topics listed above for the debating club bear witness, patriotic fervour was alive and well at St Beuno's. When war broke out in 1914 the newly-ordained clergy were eager to serve as chaplains to the forces and many of them did so. But rather oddly it is that year, 1914, in which the number of lecturers reached its peak of seven with the appointment of Leonard Geddes to teach Fundamental Theology, having been given two years at the French theologate in Hastings to prepare himself.[2] For fifty years there had been questions raised about the staffing levels and the quality of the teaching - not to mention the isolation of the theologate. Such was the shortage of teachers that in 1857 all those on the long course were sent abroad for a year.

In 1866 the Provincial was complaining about the cost of maintaining the faculty, adding that he could use the men elsewhere, while the General expressed the opinion that the whole enterprise should be moved somewhere less remote. This was the Belgian Peter Beckx. His predecessor, the Dutchman Jan Roothaan, a refugee from the civil unrest in Rome, had visited St Beuno's and planted an oak tree in 1849,[3] so perhaps in the Society's Rome headquarters there was a living memory of the College's isolation. In 1874 there was a suggestion that both the philosophers from Stonyhurst and the theologians should come together in Roehampton: "The staff, it seems, were in favour of the two faculties being combined in an impressive academic institution which could attract lay students, which would be more exciting, could offer the possibility of inviting people to disputations and give the students of one

1 Schultenover, *George Tyrrell*, p. 37. On the General's attitude to Tyrrell, see the remarkable study by David Schultenover, *A View From Rome* (New York, Fordham University Press, 1993), passim.

2 Edwards, *Canute's Tower*, p. 81f.

3 He ordered a day's holiday in perpetuity, to be held in October, a custom which survived the move to Heythrop. The requirement from January 1854 that Jesuits wear a "Roman" collar in place of the civilian attire which had been customary is also attributed to the General's visit.

faculty the opportunity of attending lectures in the other".[1] In fact those on the short course had been sent to Roehampton to join the novices in 1871, but had returned after a year.

In 1876 Alfred Weld, who had been Provincial but was now an assistant to the General in Rome, criticised the standard of the lecturers and wanted it to be discussed. A commission was eventually set up to examine the situation. John Jagger, the Prefect of Studies at St Beuno's in 1902 wrote the report: "He urged that divergent Scholastic theories should receive less attention, that the Professors should be better acquainted with the work of rationalists and be able to expound them to the students, that Higher Biblical criticism should be studied, and that more attention should be given to the historical aspects of Theology. Church history should pay more attention in a British context to the Papacy, Holy Orders etc. There should be a separate teacher of Canon Law, and there was need of men competent in Oriental languages and trained in Ecclesiastical History. The isolation of St Beuno's was deplorable. Professors can only keep in touch through magazines and reviews ... The principal conclusion was that the theologate should be moved to a place more in contact with the life of the time".[2]

Then, in 1907 Franz Xavier Wernz who, it will be recalled, had briefly taught at St Beuno's but from 1906 was General of the Society, said philosophers and theologians should be combined in one "Collegium Maximum", to be created near London or some other large city. The Provincial accepted the idea in principle, though he told the General that a move was impracticable at the time because of the cost. It was not until almost two decades later that the General's instructions were carried out and, even then, the new Collegium Maximum was located not near some big city but in the heart of the Oxfordshire countryside.

1 Edwards, *Canute's Tower*, p. 96.

2 Edwards, *Canute's Tower*, pp. 101-02

HEYTHROP COLLEGE, OXFORDSHIRE, 1926

In sharp contrast to the move of the theologians from Stonyhurst to St Beuno's, the relocation to Oxfordshire was greeted with some excitement - as Thomas Roberts's article quoted above[1] bears witness. Fr Wernz had urged the move, but it did not come until the Generalate of the Austrian-born Polish Count Wlodimir Ledóchowski,[2] elected after Wernz's death in 1915. That of course was during the First World War, and it may have been the War which delayed compliance with Wernz's instructions: that, and finding a suitable property. A "diligent search" had been made, claimed E. J. K. in 1923, but to no avail until "Mr Tipping, that most obliging and painstaking land agent in Oxford, ascertained that Mr Brassey's property at Chipping Norton was on the market".[3] What was purchased was about half the estate, plus the mansion itself, in all some 430 acres. Brassey had bought it in 1870 for £110,000 and - again according to E. J. K. - had spent the same amount again on restoring it.

The house had originally been built for Charles Talbot, the first (and only) Duke of Shrewsbury (1660-1718), who had grown to dislike his ancestral home and wanted something more befitting his status. He purchased the estate in 1697, though the house was in poor repair and, while in Italy, commissioned an architect to draw up plans. Back in England, however, he handed the commission to Thomas Archer who in turn handed the task of realising the plans to Francis Smith of Warwick, perhaps the best-known building contractor (and sometime architect) of his day: the work finally began in 1707. Charles Talbot died in 1718, and it is unlikely that either he or his wife, who survived him for eight years, ever lived at Heythrop. Both he and his Italian wife had renounced Catholicism, she to marry him, he so that he might take part in English political life. They had no children so on his death the earldom of Shrewsbury was inherited by his cousin Gilbert Talbot who was a Jesuit and consequently had to renounce it in favour of his younger brother George: Charles Talbot, afraid that Gilbert would inherit and hand the Shrewsbury

1 P. 88 fn3.

2 He governed the Society for twenty-seven years, and was renowned as a stern disciplinarian. One of his sisters has been canonised, another beatified.

3 LLNN 1923, p. 216ff., the initials apparently belonging to Edward King, who tells his readers that Heythrop is pronounced "Heethrop", and so it has remained. The Mr Brassey referred to was not the railway builder but one of his sons.

estates over to the Church, had already willed the lands on to George, insisting that they should not be alienated by a Catholic.[1]

George may have been attached to the house, but it seems his descendants were not, because they rarely lived there, though in 1829 a chapel was in the process of being built for the Catholic tenants that Catholic landowners always seemed to gather to themselves. At the time the house was leased to the Duke of Beaufort - hence the Heythrop Hunt - but in 1831 a fire destroyed much of what was reputed to have been one of the finest suite of reception rooms in England, and the Shrewsbury family moved their seat to Alton Towers. The ruins of the house remained until the purchase by Brassey who restored not only the interior of the mansion but the extensive gardens as well.[2]

Edward King was an enthusiast. Robert Butterworth, arriving at the College a quarter of a century later, was a rather more jaundiced observer:

> To the central "mansion", as we still called it, were added two wide-spreading two-storey wings, one of which surrounded the old stables and housed the philosophers; while the other, enclosing the Real Tennis court (crudely transformed into the College's main chapel), housed the theologians. There was a large self-contained estate all round the College: football pitch, cricket ground, swimming pool, nine-hole golf course,[3] tennis courts, bowling greens, deep woodlands, rockeries, waterfalls, two large lakes, a long Victorian "nature walk", even a well-filled cemetery. All this lay at the end of a forbidding, two-mile drive, which only led, in any case, to the A34, hurrying through the bleak Cotswold countryside, an unattractive and little visited region. We had no neighbours. In the College we lived in a world of our own, looking inwards...The general regime could afford to be fairly free and easy since our desert location took care of many potential disciplinary problems of the kind that would have arisen had we been living among normal human habitations.[4]

1 Cf. Stuart Handley, "Talbot, Charles, Duke of Shrewsbury (1660-1718)", *Oxford Dictionary of National Biography*, Oxford University Press, 2004, online edition accessed 8 November 2013.

2 He was also Master of the Hunt from 1873 to 1918.

3 A nine-hole golf course had been constructed at St Beuno's in the 1890s.

4 Robert Butterworth, *The Detour. Towards Revising Catholicism* (Leominster, Gracewing, 2005), pp. 94, 95.

The open-air swimming pool, it should be said, though undoubtedly decked out as such with changing rooms, was in fact a static water tank: it was the want of a nearby supply of water - despite the lakes at the bottom of quite a steep hill - which allowed the fire of 1831 to take such a devastating hold.

Butterworth's account, though evocative and representative of what many of the students may have felt, is not quite right. It was - and is - the A44 which passes by Heythrop, and it is difficult to think of the Cotswolds, one of England's most attractive regions, as either bleak or little visited. And as for Heythrop being a "desert location", it was rather less so than either Stonyhurst or St Beuno's, being only four miles to Chipping Norton in one direction, fifteen miles to Oxford in the other. It was possible to walk to Chipping Norton, though there was little or no incentive to do so. It was hardly a flourishing metropolis, not yet discovered by any particular political set. It was not really feasible to walk to Oxford on days out - Blandykes had transferred seamlessly to yet another location, as had the October "General's Day" - but certainly in the days of Butterworth's sojourn at the Collegium Maximum as a student it was still possible to "hitch a lift" along the A44 and even, as he remarks elsewhere in his autobiography, to spend the afternoon in an Oxford cinema. Transport was sometimes laid on for those with business in the town, trying on a new suit, for example, or buying the black trilby which, by some ukase of a forgotten hierarch, all clerics were expected to wear while out on the street.

In May 1924, a year or so after the estate had been purchased, Cardinal Bourne, the Archbishop of Westminster, paid a visit. "His Eminence was very favourably impressed by what he saw" was the report. A year later, under the charge of Fr Blackett and "Mr Foster, the architect, who had thoroughly entered into all our ideas and worked throughout in a spirit of perfect accord",[1] it had begun to look like the College it became. There were two wings, the theologians' to the right as one faced the building, the philosophers' to the left though when the Cardinal came there was some time to go before they were to become habitable. By that date, however, the chapel had been finished and an altar from Blackmore Park, the family seat of the Hornyolds, a long-standing

1 LLNN XLI (1926), p. 250.

recusant family whose estate was being broken up, had been installed in a small chapel at the back. As to heating, "Some will naturally regret the loss of their familiar poker ... [but] Modern central heating, as employed in the newer hotels, is a very efficient method, and the whole question has been very carefully studied".[1] The rooms were filled, as pantechnicons arrived from St Beuno's, Stonyhurst and London loaded with furniture, much of it well-worn and rickety. It was not only the buildings which had been transformed. The gardens, carefully restored by Brassey, had long been neglected and a lay brother came to tend them. The Italian garden was brought back to life and an extensive vegetable garden cultivated with such success that the produce could not only feed the very large community but was sold on the market in Oxford. The vine was thriving.

The first batch of scholastics to arrive were the philosophers, straight from their villa (holiday) in Barmouth. They were followed by the theologians, rather more in dribs and drabs, but they were all there by 23rd August 1926. So all were present, students, lecturers and administrators, when, two days later, Fr William Bodkin was installed as Heythrop's first Rector. The anonymous chronicler in *Letters and Notices* felt the need to explain, for the new man in charge had been Provincial, and had not yet completed the customary six-year term. "It was regarded on all hands as of paramount importance", he wrote, "that the extremely difficult task of the conduct of a Collegium Maximum, new alike in personnel and material surroundings, should be given to the most capable man, irrespective of the work on which he might be employed. Rome concurred".[2] Fr Bodkin responded to the toast of "The Rector". The success or failure of the enterprise, he assured the community seated together in the enormous T-shaped refectory, did not depend on the rector but on the community, *docentes et discentes*, both teachers and students.

Not all scholastics, however, had yet assembled. As they did every year the Jesuit scholastics made their eight-day retreat and only after that were they joined by those from abroad - fifty-two of them in the first year of the Collegium Maximum, seventeen from the Upper Canada Province, which was

1 LLNN XL (1925), p. 296.
2 LLNN XLI (1926), p. 249.

English-speaking and traditionally at odds with the Francophone Lower Canada. There were students from Ireland, Spain, Germany, Holland, Jugoslavia [sic], Brazil, Portugal and fourteen from three different Provinces in the United States. Even if the numbers were never quite as high again, there was usually a fairly large group of overseas students except, of course, during the war years. No doubt they came from a variety of motives, though the desire to learn English was a common theme: some were expecting to go as missionaries to countries where English was the main language or at least the language of instruction - Japan for example.

At Heythrop the language of instruction remained Latin, as it had always been, though some subjects did not lend themselves readily to translation into a dead language. It was, of course, not simply philosophy - still with a Suarezian tinge - or theology that was taught but, in the tradition of Liège and St Mary's Hall, during the years in philosophy, mathematics and the natural sciences were studied, and examined, as well. These supplementary courses, Butterworth has remarked of a somewhat later period[1] were often of greater interest than the core disciplines. Neither the system nor the timetable had much changed with the migration to the Oxfordshire countryside. "A few months later [after the move in 1926]", Paul Edwards records, and indeed regrets, "a philosopher was to write a blithe description of the move, concluding 'The life of St. Mary's Hall has been preserved intact and transplanted to Oxfordshire, and all the customs and traditions of the old regime have as far as possible been retained'".[2] Nor did Edwards think very highly of the teaching to which he was subjected: "I left Philosophy with an undeservedly high mark in 1946 having never heard the names of Ayer or Wittgenstein. I left Theology in 1956 with quite modest results, but sharing with my more successful contemporaries complete ignorance of the work of Karl Barth and a quite hazy notion of what was meant by Form Criticism".[3] It is perhaps difficult to take this quite at face value. Though Butterworth rather echoes these sentiments which may in many instances have been deserved, Frederick Copleston had

1 Butterworth, *The Detour,* p. 100.

2 Edwards, *Canute's Tower*, p. 103.

3 Edwards, *Canute's Tower*, p. 103.

been teaching for some time when Edwards was in philosophy, and he was undoubtedly well acquainted with the work of Ayer and in 1949 took part in a debate with Ayer about logical positivism on the BBC's Third Programme - Radio Three as it has since become. As for form criticism, it is again hard to believe this was not at the very least mentioned in classes for the two professors lecturing on scripture, Cuthbert Lattey and Edmund Sutcliffe, were both distinguished scholars.

Unlike most of their predecessors at St Beuno's, Lattey (1877-1954) and Sutcliffe (1886-1963) had received an appropriate training, the former during a year at Oxford under the Regius Professor of Hebrew, S. R. Driver, and the latter for three years in Rome. After the Modernist crisis of the first decade or so of the twentieth century these were difficult years for scripture scholars in particular. It was therefore quite bold of Lattey to launch into a completely new translation of the Bible, translating it from the original languages when only the Latin Vulgate was regarded by the Catholic Church as authoritative. This meant that Lattey's translation could not be used in the Catholic liturgy, despite the fact that the enterprise had the blessing of the Cardinal Archbishop of Westminster - hence the name "Westminster Version". The first part to appear, in 1913, was I Thessalonians and it contained a note on Paul's understanding of the Parousia which was criticised by the (Jesuit) American *Ecclesiastical Review* and then condemned by Rome's Biblical Commission. Lattey fell into line for the second edition, which must have been difficult for him for, as his obituary remarks, "with his simplicity there went a genuine humility, yet neither of these qualities excluded a firm confidence in his own judgment or an appreciation, at times almost naïve, of his standing in the world of scholarship".[1] Sutcliffe was the more conservative of the two, "stoutly and unashamedly conservative" his obituarist describes him, who "lectured throughout in an efficient, flexible and stylish Latin which was much appreciated by the connoisseurs but not always by those whose Latin was of a humbler variety".[2] But he was prepared to change his mind. He began his teaching career persuaded that the Gospels described Christ as having spent a three-year period preaching and teaching, but after careful study became

1 LLNN LXI, p. 168. 2 LLNN LXVIII, p. 138

convinced that he had been wrong and subsequently published *A Two Year Public Ministry*,[1] which became the first volume in "The Bellarmine Series" which Sutcliffe edited.

When Heythrop was established in Oxfordshire it was put under the religious patronage of the Jesuit theologian Robert Bellarmine (1542-1621), who had just - in 1923 - been beatified,[2] hence the name for the series of scholarly monographs, many of them by Frederick Copleston and most of them by members of the Heythrop faculty including, rather daringly for the time, *Sex Enlightenment and the Catholic* by J. E. Leycester King, which came out, as ever, from Burns and Oates, in 1944. Although James Cammack's *The Moral Problems of Mental Defect*, his doctoral thesis, had the rare distinction of being translated into Swedish,[3] perhaps the most significant of the non-Copleston publications in the series was Maurice Bévenot's *St Cyprian's "De Unitate" Chap. 4 in the Light of the Manuscripts*, also a doctoral thesis, which appeared in 1937 and established Bévenot as a leading - perhaps the world's leading - authority on the letters of the third-century martyred bishop of Carthage. Something of an expert in Latin palaeography, he went on the publish *The Tradition of Manuscripts: A Study in the Transmission of St Cyprian's Treatises* and an edition with translation of Cyprian's *De Lapsis and De Ecclesiae Catholicae Unitate*, both published by Oxford University Press.[4] Part of the significance of both these treatises of St Cyprian was the light they threw on the notion of papal primacy in the early Church,[5] and it was therefore not surprising that Bévenot lectured on ecclesiology, the theory of the Church, and that he was extremely active in the Ecumenical Movement even when participation in it was frowned upon by Rome. He became a peritus, an expert advisor, in the

1 London, Burns and Oates, 1939. Sutcliffe also compiled *Bibliography of the English Province of the Society of Jesus, 1773-1953* (London, Manresa Press, 1957) which has been much consulted in writing this history.

2 He was canonised in 1930 and declared a doctor of the Church the following year.

3 Burns and Oates, 1938. A US edition appeared the following year, and the Swedish one in 1947.

4 Strictly speaking, they were published by The Clarendon Press, the academic imprint of OUP, the former in 1961 and the latter ten years later, though there were various editions and translations.

5 Bévenot once revealed to the present writer that as a young student he wanted to study scripture but, because of the risks entailed in scholarly biblical criticism as a consequence of the Modernist crisis, he chose the rather safer field of patristics.

preparatory commission on the Church at the Second Vatican Council and a member of the Secretariat for Christian Unity.[1] In earlier, more polemical, years he had written a pamphlet *When is a Priest not a Priest: The Nature of Anglican Orders*,[2] something he came to regret.

There were a number of other serious scholars teaching at Heythrop in the period criticised by Edwards. There was Bernard Leeming, for example, who wrote a good deal about ecumenism as well as publishing an important book *Principles of Sacramental Theology*[3] which went through several editions both in Britain and in the United States. In philosophy Thomas Gornall - who, when Heythrop moved to London, went to Birmingham to assist in the massive project of editing Cardinal Newman's *Letters and Diaries* - taught natural theology: "His book *A Philosophy of God* (Darton, Longman and Todd, 1962)", Butterworth commented, "is quite the most lucid and penetrating presentation I know of scholastic Natural Theology".[4]

Nonetheless, excellent scholarship does not necessarily produce great teachers, and even when it did so, the lecturers at Heythrop, as in most scholasticates of religious orders or diocesan seminaries, were constrained by a number of factors. First of all there was the language: most lectures had to be given in Latin. Secondly there was Pius XI's Apostolic Constitution *Deus Scientiarum Dominus* ("God is Lord of Knowledge") of May 1931 which laid down in minute detail what was to be taught in ecclesiastical faculties, who was to teach it, who could study it and what degrees might be awarded after how long in the classroom. The Constitution itself was relatively short, but it was followed by a string of regulations,[5] laying down the topics to be taught

1 There is a privately printed booklet about the Bévenot family written by Laurence Bévenot, Maurice's Benedictine brother: *The Bévenot Saga*, 1982. Maurice's father, a Belgian, as a young man had fought at the Battle of Mentana when the papal Zouaves, in which he served, for the first and only time routed the troops of the nascent Kingdom of Italy.

2 Catholic Truth Society, 1946. A revised edition came out in 1953.

3 London, Longmans, 1956.

4 *The Detour*, p. 178.

5 Cf. A. Bea, "Deus Scientiarum Dominus: Its Origin and Spirit" in Gregorianum XXII (1941), pp. 445-66. An English translation of Bea's Italian is to be found in Theological Studies, Vol. 4 (1943), pp. 34-52.

and insisting that in theology Thomas Aquinas was to be the preferred author. In philosophy it was scholastic philosophy that was to be imparted. Thirdly the method of teaching remained that which has already been described: a thesis is advanced, its adversaries - their arguments all too often presented in wholly inadequate snippets - found wanting, evidence from the scriptures, the Fathers of the Church, other learned doctors and human reason brought forward, all rounded off in a neat syllogism, the whole to be re-presented by the examination candidate before his examining board consisting of three of his teachers.

For young Jesuits coming new to the College it was all accepted for what it was, the system one had to get through to progress in the Society. They knew little different and were on the whole more unquestioning than the theologians, who were generally considerably older and many of whom by the time they returned to the College had been through a degrec in some non-ecclesiastical university, often Oxford. There they had experienced a wholly different approach. Some had studied philosophy as part of the "Greats" course and consequently knew that there was more to be said for the "adversarii" of the philosophical theses than they had been given credit. They were also accustomed to writing essays rather than, as at Heythrop, answering questions, orally, in Latin and in syllogistic form to satisfy their examiners. Obviously there was an examination at the end of the three years of philosophy, but at the end of the fourth year of theology there was also the "ad gradum", to decide the candidate's status (grade)[1] in the Society, for only those who passed it could be superiors of major houses - or teach in one of the Society's theology or philosophy faculties. For the ad gradum a candidate had to reprise the whole of his philosophy course as well as theology.

It is hardly surprising that sitting in the lecture halls were rather grumpy young men in their late twenties and early thirties. One saving grace was the requirement to go into many lectures carrying in a makeshift cradle a complete set of the *Summa Theologiae* of St Thomas, behind which,and therefore out of sight of the lecturer, it was possible to read a novel, complete

1 There exists among priests in the Society the status of "Professed" and that of "Spiritual Coadjutors". It should be said that it is sometimes possible to pass from the rank of Spiritual Coadjutor to that of Professed for reasons other than academic success.

a crossword or, it was alleged, in at least one case to write a book.[1]

Inevitably over time the system relaxed. Lectures were increasingly in English, at least until Pope John XXIII's surprising encyclical *Veterum Sapientia* of February 1962, instructing that the "sacred sciences" be taught in Latin, sent the professors scurrying back to their former texts. But this was only a brief interlude. When Robert Butterworth returned to Heythrop to teach in 1967 he acknowledges that much had changed: "The old cycle of doctrinal treatises", he comments, "had been replaced by broader and more historically oriented courses for more general consumption".[2] Much of the change had been inspired by the Second Vatican Council, which had met between 1962 and 1965 and had brought to the Catholic Church a rather more open agenda, as exemplified in its documents which, for the students entering theology in its aftermath, provided another major source for reflection on doctrine. Not only had Bévenot been involved in the Constitution *De Ecclesia*, but a number of new members of staff, among them Butterworth himself, and Robert Murray SJ, had been studying in Rome while the Council was taking place and had imbibed not just the theology but also the spirit of the Council.

Not only did Vatican II bring massive changes to the sort of theology that was being taught, it also led to an experiment in the curriculum with philosophy and theology being integrated into a single course. This in turn brought a breakdown in the strict demarcation which had hitherto existed between the community of philosophers and that of theologians. Heythrop may have been isolated, but its inhabitants were not immune to the spirit of the age. Catholic Pentecostalism may not have been an English Jesuit trait, but prayer groups sprang up and more informal liturgies modified the hegemony of communal worship. The black Jesuit gown with its 'wings' was worn less and less often, and ties, rather than the Roman collar decreed by the General after his visit to St Beuno's, somehow miraculously appeared. The major motor

1 John Coventry, *Faith Seeks Understanding* (London, Sheed and Ward, 1951). Coventry had a distinguished career, becoming Provincial before returning to Heythrop in Cavendish Square to teach Greek. From this modest position he was selected as Master of St Edmund's House, Cambridge and played a large part in enabling St Edmund's to become a full College of the University.

2 Butterworth, *The Detour*, p. 177.

of change, however, was the re-invention of Heythrop, hitherto one of the Society of Jesus's "Collegia Maxima", as a Pontifical Athenaeum. The story of the Athenaeum leads directly into the story of the move from Oxfordshire isolation to relocation of the College in central London, and before recounting this step, something should be said of the daily life of students on the Heythrop estate.

The estate itself has been briefly described above.[1] It was maintained by gardeners and, to some extent, by the students themselves. This was supposed to be particularly true of the nine-hole golf course, the maintenance of which fell upon those who wished to use it, but some students who were eager gardeners lent a hand with other parts of the property. They also kept the 'nature walk', a wooded area with streams and small waterfalls, in good order. Within the nature walk there were a number of small huts, used on days free of study, to gather, drink tea, eat sausages and bacon or whatever else might be scrounged from the kitchen and generally potter, either as amateur woodsmen, or to look after the hives: bee-keeping was a popular hobby. There were football and rugby matches, and in summer cricket matches sometimes against village teams from the surrounding area. There were choirs and a group which toured surrounding villages entertaining pensioners. These last were popular events, though on the whole there was rather less integration of the Jesuit community with the local populace than there had been at St. Beuno's. Younger students had more involvement, for many of them cycled off to teach catechism on Sundays while the priests still in training motored off to say mass in distant parishes.

Occasionally grazing was leased out, and when a circus settled upon a farm at the end of the drive to the A44 as its winter quarters, the animals grazing could be quite exotic: huntsmen riding across the land would be startled to find themselves accompanied by galloping llamas. This was in the area directly in front of the house and provided some light relief for strolling Jesuits engaged in ambulatory prayer, or priests reading their office. The two lakes lay slightly further away from the main house. As at Stonyhurst the two student communities, philosophers and theologians, were kept strictly apart except on "fusion" days, and this included their use of the lakes: the upper one was

1 See above p100f.

denominated the theologians' lake, the lower one that of the philosophers. The philosophers' lake made for more attractive swimming, in hot weather more congenial than the swimming pool itself. There were fish in the theologians' lake, but few people took up angling as a hobby. There was a pleasant lawn alongside the theologians' lake, which made an excellent camping ground. Heythrop's own troop of Rover Scouts regularly ran adventure courses for scouts from around the area, some groups even came from quite distant towns and villages: the scouts could be of any religion or none. When Heythrop moved to London the Chief Executive of the Scout Association wrote a letter of thanks for the hospitality which so many generations of scouts had received in the grounds of the College.

The spacious grounds and attractive setting, the increasing number of relatively young and well-qualified lecturers, and the lack - apart from Heythrop - of any Catholic institution within the United Kingdom where students for the priesthood could study for ecclesiastical degrees encouraged some members of the staff to consider offering its facilities to members of other religious orders and to the diocesan clergy. But the immediate cause of the establishment of what became a "Pontifical Athenaeum" - a name wished upon Heythrop by the Roman Congregation of Studies - was the need to solve a problem internal to the structure of British Jesuit plans for the education of its recruits.

The Butler Education Act of 1944 had made it vastly easier for the Church to establish schools for the education of the children of the Catholic community. This in turn led to a greater demand, not just for teachers - obviously the Jesuits had been already supplying those for centuries - but for teachers with formal qualifications in education other than a university degree in classics, or history or in one of the sciences. The result was the establishment at Manresa House in Roehampton, south London, of a course of pedagogy. The idea was that this course be taken by those studying philosophy during their third year, with another year being added on in the light of the extra work required, which included teaching practice in neighbouring schools. It was not a satisfactory arrangement. It meant scholastics being removed from Heythrop, which had financial implications. It meant the library being divided between two sites at a considerable distance from each other. Most inconveniently of all it meant lecturers commuting from Oxford to London and back on a regular basis.

This structure was not sustainable. A new plan had to be drawn up and in 1957 a meeting took place at Harlaxton Manor, an extraordinary baroque construction built in the 1830s and early 1840s at the end of a mile-long drive near Grantham in Lincolnshire. The 140-room mansion had been purchased by the Society in 1947 as a novitiate[1]: the seller was the shaving-cream magnate, anti-capital punishment campaigner and spiritualist, Mrs Violet Van der Elst[2]. It was agreed at the Harlaxton meeting that the Collegium Maximum would be divided. The philosophers were to go to a new house to be built near Cambridge, the theologians were to move to Manresa House, and pedagogy was to be studied at Oxford, the course being taken after the Jesuit undergraduates had completed their degrees. This would require Campion Hall, the Oxford Jesuit house, to be extended. This last did indeed happen - which apparently caused some resentment in the rest of the English Province[3] - but not the rest of the scheme. The General of the Society, Jean-Baptiste Janssens, was a Belgian, and his own Province had just opened a Collegium Maximum at Heverlee-Leuven and was unwilling to see the British one split in two: besides, other Collegia Maxima had flourished and were having an impact nationwide within their own countries. He was also of the opinion that Cambridge was an unsuitable, because unhealthy, place for scholastics.

But if the Harlaxton plan had to be abandoned, something else had to be done to breathe life into Heythrop, to, as Fr Brinkman said, "put it on

1 On Harlaxton, see LLNN 56 (1948), pp. 203-08, reprinting an article from *Country Life* magazine for 13th October 1906.

2 She is said to have held séances in a distinctly "spooky" room, later used as the library, which, it was alleged, removal men in 1948 would not enter until it had been liberally sprayed with holy water. Harlaxton Manor was sold by the Society in 1965 to Stanford University, USA. There is an entertaining account of life at Harlaxton by Tom Shufflebotham SJ,"The Novitiate at Harlaxton Manor", LLNN 100 (2011), pp. 187-98, and see also Frank Hull SJ, "Harlaxton Manor - An Earlier Memory" in LLNN 100 (2011), pp. 317-19.

3 So alleges Bruno Brinkman in his article "The making of the Heythrop Athenaeum" (LLNN, 1998, p. 355). What is recounted here depends heavily on Brinkman's narrative, pp. 352-364, but see also Anthony Ingram, *Shepherd's Pie: Farmer into Priest* (London, Collins, 1971), pp. 118-123.

the map".[1] Bruno Brinkman was Prefect of Studies at Heythrop. His Dominican counterpart, residing at Blackfriars, Oxford, was Fr Columba Ryan. Ryan had carried out a survey on the quality of theological teaching in the religious orders in the British Isles and the results were not encouraging. There seemed here to be an opportunity for the Jesuits to put their expertise at the service of the Church and of the other religious orders who were finding it difficult to cope with the training of their own recruits. The idea was aired at a meeting in 1958 in the Dominican priory at Hawkesyard in Staffordshire.[2] Opinions were divided until the Provincial of the Passionist Fathers made a suitably impassioned speech saying "We ought to go down on our knees and thank God for the Jesuit offer"[3] to educate their students. The Passionists had a house at Broadway, within easy reach of Heythrop and in 1959 they began to commute into the College by minibus while one of their priests, Theodore Davey, started to teach canon law, remaining on the College staff from 1965 until his retirement in 2006.

News of the development spread beyond the circle of religious orders and Catholic bishops. Brinkman was interviewed by *The Times* which "informed readers in all solemnity that we were about to build the largest university in the UK"[4] on the College's nearly 500-acre site. The proposals were not everywhere as welcome as they had been to the Passionists. In a confidential report drawn up for the council of his own religious order, one superior wrote:

> Many reserves have been expressed about the Heythrop venture, especially as to the distance of the place from an urban centre, its intensely rural isolation, the dominant part played by the Society of Jesus in its conduct, the scholastic indigence of other Congregations proposing to join, as compared to ourselves, and the final character of the ecclesiastical city it might assume.[5]

---

1 Brinkman, "The Making", p. 357.

2 It was sold in 1999 and is now a nursing home.

3 Brinkman, "The Making", p. 358.

4 Brinkman, "The Making", p. 359.

5 Heythrop Archives, file headed "Administration to May 1970".

But there were others who were enthusiastic, in particular the Archbishop of Westminster who was, from September 1963, John Carmel Heenan.

Heenan's support was, as Brinkman describes it, somewhat overwhelming. He saw the College, says Brinkman as "a useful joker" in his pack. "The Heythrop scheme had become a part of his national policy-making" and having the Jesuits on his side "contributed to his own credibility, where he imagined he needed it, namely with that same bench of bishops".[1] That may have been so, but in the second volume of his autobiography *A Crown of Thorns*[2] the only mention he makes of the College is with reference to the ecumenical conference he organised there in 1962 while still Archbishop of Liverpool and to which he invited the Jesuit ecumenist Cardinal Augustin Bea, who by this time headed Rome's Secretariat for Christian Unity. Heythrop was an obvious place to hold such a gathering for it was the home of two of the country's leading academic ecumenists, Maurice Bévenot, who has already been mentioned, and the American-born Jesuit Bernard Leeming whose remarkable career had taken him as a teacher to Georgetown University, to Rome (from which he was expelled because, apparently, of derogatory remarks about Mussolini), to Ceylon (now Sri Lanka) and India before he finally settled, apart from frequent lecture tours, at Heythrop. The conference was a modest success though it evidently caused Heenan considerable embarrassment when the then Archbishop of Westminster, Cardinal William Godfrey, failed to find a guest room for Bea at his residence, Archbishop's House in London. Nor were the English bishops particularly pleased when, before the conference, Bea insisted on visiting the Archbishop of Canterbury, Michael Ramsey, at Lambeth Palace: they suspected Ramsey of having persuaded Bea, in the interests of good relations between the two Churches, to oppose the canonisation of the English martyrs. It is clear from his account that Heenan rather thought so, too.[3]

Had Heenan produced a longer autobiography he might have written more about the College, but he chose to end the account of his life in 1963 (he

1 Brinkman, *The Making*, p. 360.
2 London, Hodder and Stoughton, 1974.
3 Heenan, *Crown of Thorns*, pp. 325-29.

died in 1975), before the plan for the "Pontifical Athenaeum" had come to fruition. That event he greeted somewhat bizarrely on 25th May 1965 with a mass for school children whom he had bussed into Westminster Cathedral - he had by this time succeeded Cardinal Godfrey. On 15th June 1965, himself a Cardinal from the previous February, he was installed as Chancellor of the newly constituted Athenaeum, dressed in a robe "of some theatrical splendour".[1] The garment was based on the portrait which hung in the hall at Heythrop of Henry, Cardinal Duke of York, attired as Chancellor of the Roman Church. Brinkman delivered a Latin oration, of which a translation was made available to the no doubt grateful guests.[2]

A further task for the Cardinal Archbishop was to bless the new library, a rather ugly building with an unnecessarily vast reading room, which had been constructed to hold up to half a million volumes. Hitherto, although both the philosophers and the theologians had ready access to their own working libraries, the College's main collection had been housed in a series of cramped attics, including one locked room labelled "Hell" where works considered unsuitable for general consumption, such as Luther's *Table Talk* and a graphically illustrated edition of Rabelais, were shelved. Special permission was required by scholastics to consult this "Bibliotheca Major". This Library development was all part of the preparation for the establishment of the Athenaeum, so also was starting an academic periodical, *The Heythrop Journal*, in 1960, originally as a quarterly published by Blackwell.[3] The academic staff was bolstered by the addition of Charles Davis, who had been teaching at the Westminster diocesan seminary and who was widely regarded as the foremost Catholic theologian in Britain.[4] Planning permission was sought, and granted, for

1 Brinkman, "The Making", p. 362.

2 It was published in the *Heythrop Journal* VI (1965), pp. 387-98.

3 At the time of writing Blackwell, now Wiley-Blackwell, are still the publishers, though there was a period when the Journal was published by the College itself.

4 Natalie K. Watson, "Davis, Charles Alfred (1923-1999)", *Oxford Dictionary of National Biography*, Oxford University Press, 2004 [http://www.oxforddnb.com/view/article/71960, accessed 7 Dec 2013]. See also Charles Davis, *A Question of Conscience* (London, Hodder and Stoughton, 1967). Davis scarcely mentions Heythrop, where he taught from 1964 to 1966.

fifteen houses on the site,[1] including one for Jesuits studying philosophy: the General of the Society had belatedly decided it was not appropriate for philosophers and theologians to share the same building, albeit in two distinct wings. Two of these houses were constructed and lived in, another, for an order of nuns, was already in an advanced stage of planning before the "ecclesiastical city", and with it the idea of a Pontifical Athenaeum, was abandoned[2].

There were many reasons for the change of plan. In his account in *Letters and Notices* Bruno Brinkman lists only two. He first mentions the change in requirements for the degree taken by clerical students at Heythrop. The degrees commonly awarded, apart from the four doctorates which had already been granted by the Athenaeum, were the Licentiates in Philosophy (Lic. Phil.) and in Theology (S.T.L.). Hitherto these had taken three and four years of study respectively: now Rome decided they were to last for four and five years.[3] This was not in itself unreasonable. The "Licentiate" was technically a licence to teach, and should therefore have been the equivalent of a Masters degree. Though many of the orders and the dioceses wanted their students to have this level of competence, at least in theology, they were not prepared to add a further two years to preparation for the priesthood, with its attendant extra costs. Brinkman protested, but Rome, in the person of the Apostolic Delegate Igino Cardinale, was unmoved. Then there was a further blow. Though there was planning permission for the development of the site, it transpired there were doubts about the security of the water supply: any new houses were required to have water pumped from the nearby village. "Nearby" was a relative term: the new water main would have had to run for two miles, and cost a further £30,000. It was all too much. In 1966 there had been nine

1 When a plan was prepared of the site for the purposes of its sale, the locations of the houses already built, and of the thirteen other proposed houses, were clearly marked, together with the suggested site of an observatory. The plan is to be found in an unmarked file, the last one in the Heythrop archive.

2 One house cost £55,000, the other £110,000. Though it was not built, the house for the order of nuns still cost £30,000. The Library, completed in 1965, had cost £340,000.

3 Cf. the 1968 document from the Congregation of Catholic Studies, "Normae quaedam ad Constitutionem Apostolicam 'Deus Scientiarum Dominus' de Studiis Academicis Ecclesiasticis Recognoscendam".

religious orders who had indicated that they would like to build houses on the Heythrop site, but a year later several of them had withdrawn. There were various reasons: a general drop in vocations, the cost of building, the establishment in North London of the Missionary Institute which attracted away from the Athenaeum several orders who might otherwise have been interested. But, perhaps more importantly for the future development of the College, a good number of the younger members of the Jesuit faculty had also lost confidence in the project of a Pontifical Athenaeum.

In late October 1967 a meeting was held in the senior common room at Heythrop of the Jesuit staff. It began with Bruno Brinkman being asked by the Rector to outline the future development of the Athenaeum. He unrolled a map of the site, and pointed out where the future halls of residence were to be built. After he had finished the Rector then announced that an alternative plan was being considered, one which would move the College closer to a state university. This apparently sudden turn of events caused considerable debate among those present - and indeed, among some members of staff aroused considerable alarm.[1] Robert Butterworth, who was present, describes it in his memoirs:

> The Rector, William Maher - always known as Johnny - had taught me at Preston when I was eleven years old. A man of instinctive intelligence and elemental energy, it was he who first aired the idea of closing down Heythrop and moving the Athenaeum elsewhere. In the senior community there was considerable upset and consternation. The lid we had all been keeping on the problem brewing within the Athenaeum had been lifted, and it was never to be replaced. Factions immediately surfaced among the staff, and there was active lobbying for and against the closure. At least one of the older members, Freddie Copleston, the distinguished historian of philosophy, sided with the younger element, and this, I believe, proved decisive in the end.[2]

Copleston, it ought perhaps to be explained, was a very sociable individual,

1 John Mahoney, LLNN 99 (2009).

2 Butterworth, *The Detour*, pp. 178-9

though not necessarily with his Jesuit confrères,[1] and he found his social life more restricted in Oxfordshire than it was during the half year he spent annually at the Gregorian University in Rome. His views certainly added considerable weight to the endeavours of the younger members of staff who signed a letter to Fr Maher urging the move.

A number of reasons have already been indicated for the apparent change of heart on the part of the Jesuit authorities. As the Jesuit Treasurer was later to write, Heythrop in Oxfordshire was not financially viable with less than 250 students, and there were only 150.[2] It had, moreover, become clear at two meetings in September and October that it was unlikely more non-Jesuit students would be sent to the Athenaeum. In the September meeting which was with the four Archbishops of England and Wales, the Archbishops expressed their misgivings about putting up a house for diocesan clergy. The October gathering was of Provincials of other religious orders who all had similar doubts. The Jesuit Provincial was of the opinion that they were hesitant to build because they would be doing so on the Society's property and on 15th June 1966 he therefore announced the setting up of an independent trust to which the Society would convey the entire Heythrop estate so that it would no longer be Jesuit territory. This remarkably generous proposal - which was overtaken by events - was interpreted by one Catholic newspaper as meaning that the Jesuits were leaving Heythrop.

1 Among Copleston's many letters preserved in the archives of Boston College there is only one from an English Province Jesuit. "When, in advanced years, I look back on my life, what I chiefly regret is my lack of real love for those with whom I have been in contact ... It is a failure in Christian love which lies most heavily on my own conscience, a failure which has manifested itself in my relations with and attitudes to members of my family, friends and acquaintances, fellow-Jesuits and others". This quotation comes from the final chapter of the original text of his *Memoirs*. A quite different version appeared in print. The original version is to be found in the Copleston archive at Boston College. Unfortunately no reference can be given. As the archivists had not realised it was among the papers which Copleston had deposited, this particular Mss had not been catalogued. An essay on Copleston by the present author and largely based on the Boston College archive will appear in a volume to be published by Gracewing and provisionally entitled *Catholic Clerical Scholars of the Twentieth Century*. It is to be edited by Martin John Broadley, PhD., a priest of the Salford diocese and former student at Heythrop.

2 Heythrop archives, file headed "Correspondence prior to the London move". This was true of Heythrop in Oxfordshire whether or not there had been the Athenaeum.

A memorandum was prepared for the Advent meeting of the Bishops' Conference of England and Wales on 10th December 1967. It argued both cases, that of staying put and that of moving into the campus of some English university. On 29th February 1968 at a meeting at Archbishop's House, Westminster, it was agreed to set up a working party to consider the implications of a move. At the first meeting of the working party, held at Farm Street, the Jesuit headquarters in London, five universities were proposed as possible sites for Heythrop: Oxford, Bristol, Nottingham, Manchester and London. The second meeting, on 27th June 1968, settled on London, only a little more than half a year since the proposal of a move had first been mooted. "Johnny" Maher's "elemental energy" had clearly been put to good use.

Although five universities had been mentioned (Gordon Wheeler, the Bishop of Leeds, had also suggested Leeds, but he himself eventually advised against), ultimately it came down to a choice between Manchester and London: Oxford would have required the College to move to within three miles of Carfax, the central point of the city, and a new building would have to be constructed or acquired; Bristol's theology department was simply too small; Nottingham does not appear to have been seriously considered. Manchester's offer was excellent, but London was eventually decided upon for a variety of reasons: the Athenaeum was thought to be of national importance, and therefore ought to be in the nation's capital; there were a good many religious houses already located in London, so the orders would find it less expensive to find accommodation for their students; London was judged to be more attractive than Manchester to lay students, a very small number of whom had already studied at Heythrop in the country; there would be greater ecumenical contact, more openings for apostolic work and more opportunities to attend cultural events.[1]

It is not immediately obvious that all of these reasons for preferring London over Manchester were equally valid, and there is one which goes unmentioned though it is difficult to believe it did not weigh heavily with those negotiating the move: unlike Manchester, London was a collegiate university. In other words, Heythrop as such could retain its identity. This was

1 These reasons are listed in Heythrop archives file headed "University Negotiations".

important for the "Athenaeum", the papal university, which is what, at least at first, the negotiators believed they were bringing to London. The Congregation for Catholic Education were asked to approve the move and did so in a letter to the President of the Athenaeum, the Jesuit Provincial, dated 25th July 1968: "a link with a civil university is desired by all for the fuller academic and apostolic formation of its students". [1] A formal application was made to the University of London on 8th February 1969, asking that Heythrop be accepted as a school of the University in the Faculty of Theology. Drawing up the application, however, had not been without difficulty. An early draft of this document survives to which, in December 1971, Copleston attached a note:

> This draft is extremely interesting. It is based on the assumption that the University was being asked to consider the recognition of the Pontifical Athenaeum as a school of the University, and that in the event of acceptance Heythrop students could obtain both a University degree and a Pontifical degree for basically the same set of studies ... It looks as though the document was based on an important misunderstanding.[2]

Well, perhaps so, but there is ample evidence, of which Copleston would have been aware, that the original idea had been to first present students who needed a licentiate, clerics, that is, who were possibly going on to teach in seminaries, for a London degree in theology, and this would be followed by a year or so extra of more Church-related instruction to qualify for the licentiate.

Before the formal letter of application was sent there had, of course, already been preliminary negotiations, much helped by the fact that Bishop Gordon Wheeler had been a friend from Oxford days of the University's Principal, Sir Douglas ("Jock") Logan. One of the first things the University needed to know was whether there would be, in London, appropriate accommodation for teaching: on 16th December 1968 Johnny Maher offered some of, and potentially the whole of, the Jesuit London headquarters at Farm Street and Mount Street in Mayfair. The sisters of the Society of the Holy

1 Heythrop archive, "University Negotiations": "Nexus cum universitate civili ab omnibus desideratur ad ampliorem formationem alumnorum academicam et apostolicam".

2 Heythrop archive, "University Negotiations".

Child Jesus had, however, been running a graduate training college at numbers 11 to 13 Cavendish Square, two elegant Georgian buildings joined by a bridge over Deans Mews. It was about to close, and this was offered to the College for a reasonable rent as a home. The offer was gratefully taken up for a relatively modest rent, and this was the property that was inspected when on the 8th and 9th May 1969 the University of London sent a team to visit Heythrop in Oxfordshire and, on the following day, the proposed location in Cavendish Square. It was not simply Cavendish Square, however. Part of the plan was to locate the Library in nearby Binney Street, but to this the inspectors objected: the Library, they insisted, should be on the main site. Otherwise the report was very positive, though some doubts remained about the financial viability of the new College, and the Clerk of the Court visited the Provincial to discuss the issue. The following day, 16th July 1969, the Provincial, Fr Terence Corrigan wrote to the Clerk:

> I wish to thank you for the courtesy of your visit yesterday at which we discussed the financing of the Heythrop College, London. I write to confirm that the Society of Jesus underwrites this undertaking and have agreed to make good whatever financial deficiencies may be incurred, and thus insure [sic] its viability from our own financial resources.[1]

On that same day, 16th July 1969, the Senate of the University announced that it had decided to admit Heythrop as a School of the University in the Faculty of Theology.

Much, of course, still had to be done. One major issue was the sale of Heythrop Hall in Oxfordshire with its many acres. This did not prove at all problematic. There were several expressions of interest, including one from an American university, and in October 1969 it was sold to the National Westminster Bank as a training college for their employees: it afterwards became a hotel and conference centre. Another matter of concern was integrating Heythrop's course of studies with that of the University of London. There were highly satisfactory meetings with members of the faculty of theology at

1 Heythrop archives, "Provincial 1969-1976".

King's College (until Heythrop received its charter after a probationary year, the College's undergraduates had to be registered with the University through King's) which showed to the satisfaction of academic staff that there were aspects of the curriculum such as sacramental theology and ecclesiology where they could make a very positive contribution. All seemed well - but there was one major issue. Rome's Congregation for Catholic Education had been delighted by the acceptance of the College into the University of London, and on 3rd October 1969 had written to say so. They were still under the impression that the Pontifical Athenaeum had been received under Senate House's umbrella. As has been remarked above, there had been talk of the licentiates continuing, simply by the addition of some extra studies to the London degree, but the University completely rejected the idea. If the Athenaeum was to survive at all, and they would rather that it did not, the University authorities wanted it to be quite separate from the college itself. An accommodation address was therefore provided - the Jesuit headquarters in Mount Street - but the Athenaeum was otherwise forgotten about, at least by Heythrop. Not, however, by Rome. Copleston wrote as Principal to the Provincial on 25th April 1970:

> In point of fact the Pontifical Athenaeum is an embarrassment. I recently received, via the Apostolic Delegacy, a sixth questionnaire from the Congregation of Catholic Education. I have not the nerve to tell the Congregation bluntly that the Athenaeum has a Chancellor, a Vice Chancellor, two Deans, two Vice Deans, but no students.[1]

The Congregation did not give up. Questionnaires kept coming, and with them invitations to meetings in Rome. Butterworth went to one:

> The conference only revealed how completely out of touch the Vatican had become with the multitude of different forms which Catholic establishments had assumed over the years, and with the variety of staffing and working conditions that obtained within them. The Vatican still thought, for instance, that it could exercise a prior veto on any staff appointment anywhere, as if labour laws and trades unions and equal opportunities did not exist.[2]

1 Heythrop archives, "Administration, Heythrop to May 1970".

2 Butterworth, *Detour*, p. 180.

It was an odd thing for him to write because, as he records, Butterworth rather collided with those laws and trade unions himself. Heythrop as a college of the University of London proved to be a rather different entity than Heythrop as a Jesuit-run Pontifical Athenaeum.

Heythrop College, Chipping Norton, Oxfordshire, 1926-1970

Heythrop College, Cavendish Square, London, 1970-1993

Rev Maurice Bévenot SJ (1897-1980), who taught ecclesiology at Heythrop College in Oxfordshire and at Cavendish Square and was a consultor to the Secretariat for Unity

Rev Frederick Copleston SJ (1907-1994), author of the "History of Philosophy" and founding principal of Heythrop College, University of London, 1970-1974

Rev Theodore Davey CP,
who taught canon law at
Heythrop College, 1965-2006

Rev Brendan Callaghan SJ
(Principal, 1985-1997,
Acting Principal 1998-1999)

Heythrop College, Kensington, London, 1993 - present day

Students and Prospective Students, 2012

HEYTHROP COLLEGE, LONDON W1, 1970

A press release dated 2nd October 1970 announced the arrival of Heythrop in Cavendish Square. This occasion was not without its public drama: *The Times'* religious correspondent had filed a story which seemed to suggest that the Roman Catholic Church had opened a new College as part of the University of London. This immediately set off alarm bells and Sir Douglas Logan as Principal of the University and Frederick Copleston as Principal of Heythrop wrote a joint letter in response, which appeared on 5th October. It deserves to be quoted because the precise nature of Heythrop's Catholic identity was a recurring matter of debate:

> The University has also insisted that the college, prior to admission, must become an independent legal entity and its petition for a Royal Charter is now under consideration by the Privy Council ... If the Charter is granted[1] the college will operate under its charter in all respects as to its government, as to the admission of students and as to the relationship between members of staff and the governing body, in the same manner as any other school of the University. The religious affiliation of the college will be reflected only in the sense that its teaching will be concerned with the particular Roman Catholic contribution which can be made to the development of theological studies in the University of London.

This may have settled the question for the time being but, as will be seen, on the issue of the College's relationship to the Catholic Church the newly-installed Principal and at least some of the members of staff did not agree.

It is perhaps now hard to comprehend the excitement which the entry of the College into the University caused within the Catholic community. One distinguished Catholic priest wrote that the move was "possibly the most important event in English Catholicism for a hundred years".[2] There are now a number of foundationally Catholic institutions which have become part of the Higher Education sector while retaining much of their Catholic character

1 It was granted on the 14th of May 1971. A fortnight later two copies of the Charter were sent to the Congregation for Catholic Education.

2 Heythrop archive, file headed "Correspondence prior to the London move". The letter was dated 3rd August 1969.

but Heythrop was the first. An historian of Catholic education might see it as the logical culmination of the 1944 Education Act.

Part of the "Catholic" contribution would clearly have to be reflected in the syllabus to be studied by students at Heythrop. Before the move, which was achieved, physically, with impressive speed and efficiency, there had obviously been a planning committee and, as a subdivision of that, there was a Curriculum Committee. This was chaired by John (Jack) Mahoney, a future Principal of Heythrop in London. In an article for *Letters and Notices* he contrasted the syllabus at pre-London Heythrop to that pursued in Cavendish Square:

> The early coverage of scholastic philosophy was systematic and aimed at all the disciplines converging for the purpose of equipping students to study theology. In London in principle this systematic interconnection and subordination of philosophical disciplines, and the scholastic approach, disappeared, and the branches of philosophy were now all treated autonomously and quite independently of each other. In theology the most obvious contrast between the old and the new Heythrop approaches was in dogmatic theology (in London, christian doctrine), which was treated thoroughly and in its entirety at the old Heythrop, in comparison with the much more selective approach in London. Here there was initially only one compulsory dogma paper in the BD degree (Christian Doctrine I), although the possibility was introduced of adding as the optional papers in the BD the further christian doctrine papers devised by Heythrop, something which proved especially suitable for ordinands. By contrast, the coverage of scripture in London was more substantial and systematic than it had been in the old Heythrop and the texts covered for exegesis were more extensive, although still only a small portion of the whole canon. Students were now being provided with a fuller scriptural background, with compulsory Greek, and introduced to an explicit method of detailed exegesis of the original text which they could then apply to other texts.[1]

1 Jack Mahoney, "Heythrop's Move to London, 1970. A Personal Reminiscence", LLNN 99 (2009), pp.234-35.

As Mahoney goes on to explain, the London syllabus did not provide adequate theological formation for students for the priesthood, and courses in moral theology and canon law had to be added, as well as some liturgical studies.

Another major change was in the method of instruction. At the "ranch", as Heythrop-in-the-country came to be called, teaching had been lecture-intensive. In London there were fewer lectures but more essays, in theory one a week to be handed to a tutor. This was rather an odd provision, more reminiscent of Oxbridge - where many of the lecturers had studied - than it was of London, but it was much appreciated by the students. One long-standing member of the Heythrop faculty grumpily remarked to the present author that the undergraduates were being over-taught, but if so the results were impressive, Heythrop students regularly matching, if not surpassing, the results obtained by students from the other colleges.

There was another major mark of difference between Heythrop and the other colleges of London - or any other - university: the planning committee decided not to use titles such as professor or reader, a practice which continued until very recent times. Various reasons were advanced for this. Certainly one of them was the difficulty of deciding who should get which title. A good many of the fifteen Jesuits who transferred to London with the College would have qualified to be a senior lecturer or reader, if not professor, in any other similar institution, and it would have been invidious to pick out some rather than others. In 1972 Copleston, the College's Principal, was granted by the Senate of the University the personal title of Professor - and Professor Emeritus on his retirement - but this was a decision of the University at the request of the College, and not an appointment by the College itself, and so did not offend against the general rule.

The one exception to this self-denying ordinance was the post of Librarian. In his *Letters and Notices* article Mahoney remarks "on the proposal of one of the University governors, as Jesuit purely nominal salaries were being considered it was agreed that the College library was so important that the post of librarian should be considered equivalent to that of a university reader"[1].

1 Mahoney, "Heythrop's Move", p. 236.

This decision was precipitated by the withdrawal from the College, on reaching the University of London's retirement age, of the then Librarian, a Jesuit. It had been one of the intentions of the Planning Committee that all posts should henceforward be advertised. In order to advertise the post of Librarian it was necessary for the College to decide upon a salary, whether real or notional,[1] for the post, and it was agreed that for the office of Librarian the status of Reader was the most appropriate, as being comparable to the status conferred on the Librarian in other small institutions.

The policy of advertising posts was adhered to even when there was an appropriate Jesuit. The competition was open and, on one occasion, a potential lecturer who was a Jesuit was rejected by the interviewing panel. An early appointment through this process was to the Department of Biblical Studies, when a female Baptist minister applied, and was selected. She was chosen on her merits, though there was the obvious benefit of highlighting the College's ecumenical credentials. Improved ecumenical contacts had been one of the reasons for moving from Oxfordshire isolation, but shortly after Heythrop arrived in Cavendish Square, Richmond College, a Methodist foundation, and New College, a Congregationalist (later United Reformed) one, withdrew from the University, the former in 1972, the latter five years later. Dr Marcus Ward, of Richmond College, joined Heythrop on a part- time basis and fitted in well: he was, as he described himself, - 'a high church'- Methodist. He became a much-loved lecturer in the Department of Biblical Studies, and a prize was created in his memory[2].

There was yet another very distinctive feature about the early years of Heythrop. Jesuits for the most part live in communities where they possibly can. The Jesuit students were spread out among several London residences of the Society, especially at Southwell House located on Fitzjohn's Avenue in Hampstead. The College staff, on the other hand, or most of them, were at first accommodated in a number of mews houses immediately behind the

1 Jesuits themselves did not receive an actual salary.

2 He joined the staff on his retirement, shortly before his College withdrew from the University. Jack Mahoney has commented, in a private communication, that he was the only member of the college staff to begin his lectures with a prayer.

College, and ate together at lunch and dinner. There were College guest nights where those invited to dine were treated to a meal prepared by a quite extraordinarily (for a religious community) competent chef who swiftly proved himself both innovative and too expensive: the chef departed in September 1973.

Indeed, it was all proving too expensive. In *Detour* Robert Butterworth puts it like this:

> All went well enough until a couple of contracted staff left the priesthood to live in the lay state, and so had now to be paid their full salaries. This put a heavy strain on the College's limited resources, but their contracts gave them tenure, and they refused to resign. The rest of the staff then divided into two factions. On the right there was a feeling of outrage that the defectors did not have the decency to see the religious and financial embarrassment they were causing and withdraw from the College, and on the left there was a feeling that they had the legal right, firmly based on their tenured contracts, to keep their jobs. The split became obvious, and it was known whose side everyone was on ... Heythrop had quickly turned into an unhappy ship with a deeply divided crew.[1]

This narrative undoubtedly reflects feelings in the College at the time, but conflates two quite distinct events. Butterworth quite rightly places the major problems within the College to the 'late '70s', but the two he mentions who resigned from the priesthood did so much earlier. There was also the issue that Rome in an instruction of 1971 refused to allow priests who had returned to the lay state to continue to teach in Catholic institutions of higher education attended by seminarians. Heythrop did not fall into this category as it was not, legally speaking, a Catholic institution, but Cardinal Heenan could not be so easily appeased. It would, however, have been impossible to terminate the lecturer's contract[2] without the wrath of the Association of University Teachers,

1 Butterworth, *Detour*, pp. 195-196.

2 Only one of the two taught at the College. The other (the present author) was the Librarian to whom Rome's ruling did not apply.

the lecturers' trade union, falling upon the College. Maher came up with the solution of sending him on a sabbatical, perhaps in the hope that he would not return but, if he did choose to return (as he did), Heenan might have relented. In fact he had died, to be replaced as Archbishop of Westminster by Cardinal Basil Hume who was much more sympathetic to the individual's position. He thought it a mistake not to use the expertise of former clergy to the benefit of the Church but felt himself, given his prominent position, not able to say so publicly.

But all was not financially well before the two staff members left the priesthood and started to receive a full salary. Maher did not serve as Principal for many months before he had to relinquish the position because he was named Provincial of the English Province. In that capacity he was President of the College and in a statement to the governors on 15th September 1978 he said "The fact is that by 1972 the College's expenses were already beyond forecasts"[1] - and that was long before either of the two staff members resigned from the priesthood. There are indications in the files that although one Province Treasurer thought Heythrop-in-London to be more economic than Heythrop-in-Oxfordshire, the accountants were concerned about the financial situation even before the move. This perception is borne out by a letter of February 1974 from David Hamlyn, Professor of Philosophy at Birkbeck College and the chair of governors, to Copleston: "It is clear to me that the College was set up in London under serious misapprehensions about the financial consequences and whatever happens those mistakes must be made good. If they are not I shall have no recourse but to resign and I shall do so in a way that makes clear why I am doing so."[2]

Part of the problem lay with the terms on which Heythrop had entered the University. At the time there was a government grant to the whole University -Imperial College being an exception - which was "top sliced", as the phrase was, to provide for central services. The residue was then divided out among the University's constituent colleges. It was clear that the University would not wish to have a further call upon its resources, so Heythrop joined it as a non-grant receiving institution, though its students could claim a grant from

1 Heythrop archive, Provincial Statement.

2 Boston College archive, Copleston papers, box 11, file 1.

their local education authority to cover all, or part, of their maintenance and tuition fees. These grants were mandatory, not discretionary as they might have been with some other non-university colleges, but because there was no government grant to Heythrop some authorities believed it fell within the discretionary sector: it became a regular task for the Registrar to chase up the fees on behalf of the students. There was, nonetheless, a large funding gap, as Hamlyn pointed out in the letter just quoted, which had to be made good by "the Providing Body", as the Province was called in the parlance of the governors.

It should perhaps be explained in parentheses, as it were, that the only part of the College not suffering from the financial crisis was the Library which, as the University required by the terms of Heythrop's admission, was gradually being reassembled in Cavendish Square from its interim storage space at Stamford Hill and Osterley. The acquisitions budget for the Library had been constituted by the royalties received for their publications by members of the Heythrop staff. In practice, this meant Frederick Copleston's royalties from his history of philosophy volumes, which at the time the College joined the University amounted to some £5,000 a year. There had been a suggestion that the Library should simply be handed over to the College governors, but for various reasons this was not acceptable. The next proposal was that the new acquisitions would belong to the College, whereas all purchases before 1970 would remain the property of the Society of Jesus. This, it was pointed out by the Librarian, would lead to endless confusion, and enormous problems if the College were to close. It was decided, therefore, that the Library's contents would remain the possession of the Society, though on permanent loan, while administrative costs would be borne by the College. Eventually the Society decided to commute the royalties into a fixed sum, which would rise in subsequent years by the rate of inflation. This structure, according to which the College does not own its own Library, may well be unique in British institutions of higher education, but it has worked well and at those periods of financial stringency, such as afflict almost all colleges from time to time, has ring-fenced the budget for the acquisition of books and periodicals.

But the Providing Body had its own concerns. Although, in the letter quoted above,[1] it had committed itself to underwriting the College, it needed to ensure that the College was spending its grant from the Society in ways that furthered in some sense the Society's purposes. These purposes might have been widely defined, but they nonetheless existed, and this caused a tension within the faculty. In this debate there was no doubt where Copleston stood. In May 1973 he wrote to Hamlyn offering his resignation because of age, but he added:

> As you have doubtless divined for yourself, I have always hoped that the College would move further away from affiliations which, in my opinion, are unfavourable to its development as an autonomous School of the University, devoted to contributing as much as possible to the academic life of the University. Though however the College is certainly making a serious contribution to theological studies in the University, discussion arising out of the Murray Report[2] has made clear to me the extent to which the College in general wishes to maintain its traditional affiliations. I do not myself think that this policy is very likely to contribute to the longevity of the College. My point is however that if the College wishes to retain as long as possible its links with the Jesuit Order, and if it wishes to extend its services to the Catholic community at large (as distinct from the more strictly University aspects of its work), a Principal who would represent and develop this line of policy more wholeheartedly than I can would be wholly desirable.

Hamlyn replied to this letter nine months later, "I have been aware for some time that a substantial part of the College does not really agree with the things you have in mind, much as I myself agree with what you think". Copleston submitted to the Murray Committee a memorandum in which he outlined the future of the institutions which did not receive direct government funding. These institutions were mainly, though not only, colleges teaching denominational theology. He believed that the anomaly of non-grant receiving

1 See above p.120.

2 A report into the governance of the University of London. Its secretary was Frederick Copleston's brother Earnest, who took on the task after his retirement as Secretary of the University Grants Committee, the forerunner of the Higher Education Funding Council.

schools of the university should be ended and the theological schools brought together in a central Institute of Religious Studies. He expressed his views in "Theology: A Way Ahead", an article which appeared in the *University of London Bulletin*[1] early in 1974. "Given dictatorial powers", he wrote, "I would merge the existing Faculty of Theology in a wider Faculty or area of Religious Studies", and added "If a prospective ordination candidate chooses to make use of the facilities provided in any case by the University, that is his affair. It certainly does not follow that the University should finance additional courses of study which this or that Church considers necessary for ordinands". But there was never any likelihood of the money being available for such an enterprise, as there wasn't for the theological schools, nor was there any inclination on the part of the staff of the surviving theological schools, King's College and Heythrop, to merge in this way.

Copleston retired at the end of the academic year 1973-74. He was moving to another Jesuit institution, the University of Santa Clara in California, where he spent many happy semesters teaching part-time. California proved a useful point of departure - or return - for his voyages to the East for he was, until his eighties, an inveterate traveller. As he then wrote in his *Memoirs* "I have now lost all inclination to leave my own country", adding, "Nor am I any longer prepared to cope with the effort to speak a foreign language".[2] But when he left Heythrop he had several years of active life ahead of him, and was touched by the presentation on 14th June 1974 on behalf of the College's Students' Union by the Union's then President, T. Frank Kennedy SJ, later Canisius Professor of Music at Boston College. The gift was a pair of swimming trunks in red, white and blue which, as Kennedy later remarked,[3] in the time before the internet made such searches a good deal simpler, took a great deal of finding. Along with the swimming trunks, Kennedy assured Copleston, there was a colour-co-ordinated surf board awaiting him at Santa Clara. Copleston may have been at odds with at least some of the faculty over policy, but he was much loved and admired by the students.

1 14 Jan 1974 pp. 9-11.

2 Copleston, *Memoirs*, pp. 192-193.

3 In a private email to the author.

Not that there were many of them. When the College opened in London the total number of students was 104. Most of these were male members of religious orders, including Jesuits, 89 of them. There were seven female religious and one layman. There were four diocesan clergy and three "other religious". In the entry for September 1974 the total was 158. The number of male religious had dropped by one while female religious had risen sharply to 21. The number of lay people had also increased significantly to 20 men and 22 women, while "other religious" had declined to one. The number of diocesan clergy had also increased, but only marginally: there were now six.

There were no doubt a variety of reasons for the low take-up of places by the English and Welsh bishops. Though there was instituted what was called 'the College course' by which candidates for the priesthood might prepare themselves through the study of philosophy as required of seminarians for the basic Bachelor of Divinity degree, many of those offering themselves for the Catholic ministry did not have the required standard of education at secondary level to enter a university course. At the same time there was also a massive decline in young men offering themselves to the bishops for training, and that led on to another problem which faced the hierarchy: they had difficulty in filling their own seminaries - indeed two of them, the English College in Lisbon, Portugal, and Upholland College in Liverpool closed as major seminaries in the mid-1970s.[1]

Heythrop, of course, was not a seminary, but that did not prevent the Catholic hierarchy worrying about its Roman Catholic orthodoxy if they were to send their students to the College. George Patrick Dwyer, the Archbishop of Birmingham, wondered how orthodoxy was to be preserved in the context of the University of London. As Mahoney remarks, the issue as such never came up. And he adds: "the only teacher at Heythrop who has been officially considered with disfavour or censure by the Vatican for his theological views has been, ironically, myself, but that applied to my published writings which appeared after my retirement from Heythrop".[2] Nonetheless there remained a lingering

1 A further seminary, Ushaw College just outside Durham to which the seminarians from Upholland migrated, has since closed, though it survives as an appendage to the University of Durham.

2 Jack Mahoney, "Heythrop's Move to London", Part II (LLNN 99, 2010), p. 326.

suspicion and the problem over the priest lecturer who wished to return to the lay state did not help. Heenan let it be known that if the former priest was not removed from the College he would remove his students and, he intimated, other bishops and religious superiors would act similarly. He said this despite the fact that he had moved his seminarians from Ware in Hertfordshire to London precisely so that they might, if appropriately qualified, attend Heythrop.

As has been seen, this threat was never implemented, but in the context of a continuing financial crisis it had to be taken seriously. But then there came another challenge to the College's development, and from an unexpected source. Heythrop's admission to the University was for a trial period of five years. When the five years were over it was formally approved as a University of London College at a meeting of the University Court on 14th May 1976. Originally Heythrop had been admitted as a school in the Faculty of Theology. On 15th May 1974 it had also been admitted to the Faculty of Arts so that it might teach for the combined degree in Philosophy and Theology, for the MA degree in Philosophy, and for the BA degree in Religious Studies. Philosophy, under the particularly able stewardship of Gerard J. Hughes SJ, flourished as perhaps never before. At Heythrop in Oxfordshire the discipline had been for much of the time - though rather less so towards the end - largely subordinated to Theology. As the phrase had it, Philosophy was "the handmaid of Theology" at the "ranch", whereas in London it was most definitely a subject in its own right, and one which attracted an increasing number of students, not least because the teaching was so successful. Though the original pitch of the College had been to Catholic students, as the list of addresses to which the prospectus was sent bears witness, those drawn to Philosophy came increasingly from a variety of backgrounds. In itself no one regarded this as a problem. What was more problematic was that Philosophy was beginning to overshadow Theology.

This was not what the Jesuit superiors had envisaged when the College moved to London. The crisis, which had begun in 1974, reached its peak during the academic year 1980-1981. Maher, now Provincial, expressed his dissatisfaction with the way the College was developing. It had not overcome the suspicions of the hierarchy about its Catholic orthodoxy, indeed, about its identity. There was also disappointment on the part of Jesuit superiors that Heythrop was not playing a more active part in the "formation" (as distinct from the education) of younger members of the Society - though nothing in the discussions preparatory to the move to London appear to suggest that it should have any such role. But as the British Province was being called upon to pay an ever-increasing amount of money to keep the College in existence, it was obviously felt by some that the College should demonstrate a greater commitment to the aims of the Society. There was a serious danger that the Province would withdraw, or at least reduce, its funding, in which case Heythrop would no longer be viable.

There had been quite serious efforts to diversify the College's Catholic outreach. Part of the agreement, when it moved into the former graduate training college at Cavendish Square, was that there would be a Department of Religious Education, run by the Holy Child nuns who owned the property. When they had examined more closely all that was entailed by this proposal, however, the nuns withdrew. There had also been long negotiations about incorporating a national Liturgical Institute backed by the hierarchy, but this, too, came to nothing. Then there was the suggestion of an association with what was then called the Linacre Centre for Healthcare Ethics,[1] founded by the hierarchy in 1977, whose first research officer and later director was a Heythrop alumnus, but the Linacre Centre and the College, it was decided, had rather different approaches to bioethics. Heythrop did, however, for some years house the Linacre library.

In the midst of the crisis the governors decided upon a direct appeal to the Catholic bishops in the person of Cardinal Hume, who had shown himself very supportive of the College. The Cardinal was in Rome, and there was a dramatic, apparently last-ditch, flight to Rome by the chair of governors on 19th October 1980, but Hume could offer no serious assistance on behalf of the hierarchy beyond expressions of good will. The governors therefore came to the conclusion that if the College was to survive they had no alternative but to reduce the cost of staffing by terminating the contracts of those - there were seven in all - who were receiving full salaries. A further complication was

1 Later the Anscombe Bioethics Centre.

the prediction that academic salaries were likely to rise sharply over the coming few years, as indeed they did. Three of those affected by the governors' decision were members of a union, the Association of University Teachers (AUT), to which they appealed, and with which there were some inconclusive negotiations: Jack Mahoney foresaw what he described as a "bloody battle" with the AUT. In the event three salaried members of staff withdrew from the College voluntarily, but a letter was drawn up terminating the contracts of the remaining four at the end of the academic year, 30th September 1981.

Alternatives were suggested, such as closing the College to new students in October 1981 and for the next couple of years so that it might reopen on a new basis. Staff could then be made redundant rather than dismissed, but this idea was not given much consideration. The governors seemed determined on their policy of dismissal, a situation which was also facing universities and university departments around the country. Heythrop was in danger of being a test case and the Catholic press, which had got word of the crisis, expressed dismay - as did the "Letters to the Editor" columns. Then, somewhat belatedly and after careful study of the College's Charter, Mahoney came to the conclusion, of which he promptly informed the chair of governors, that the board had no right to dismiss staff simply on financial grounds.[1]

It was a remarkable turn-around. Robert Butterworth, who had been chosen as College Principal to replace John Mahoney who was retiring from the post, decided he 'had no future at Heythrop' and moved to a post in what is now, but wasn't then, the University of Roehampton. His decision to pull out, Butterworth added, did the College a favour.[2] Indeed the whole crisis itself did the College a favour. The Province not only kept funding the short-fall in Heythrop's finances, encouraged perhaps by a letter of Pedro Arrupe, the much-admired Jesuit Superior General, to the Provincial saying "I judge [Heythrop] the most important single endeavour of the Province",[3] but it also

1 Cf. Mahoney, "Heythrop's Move" Pt II, pp. 331-333. See also documents in the Heythrop Archive file headed "Fr Maher's correspondence".

2 Butterworth, *Detour*, p. 197.

3 Letter dated 25th March 1977 to be found in the Heythrop Archive file headed "Fr Maher's correspondence": Arrupe had been kept informed of the problems of the College.

put the College's finances on a more stable basis. Members of staff may not have been immediately aware of this, but they were certainly aware of the Province's commitment when it drafted six more Jesuits into the College and opened an Institute of Spirituality which proved a considerable draw for more mature students. Brendan Callaghan, who later took over as Principal, began a degree in the psychology of religion, the first in the country, which, too, attracted a considerable clientele. The Academic Board started to give more thought to the financial aspects of its programme and began to develop a range of Masters Degrees, which could be studied either full-time or part-time. These courses, and in particular the Postgraduate Diploma in Pastoral Theology, originally conceived of as a means of providing the fourth year of theology Jesuits were expected to undertake, proved to be attractive to a large and diverse student body[1] and, in time, the fees relieved pressure on Heythrop's finances.

Almost from the start, Heythrop in London had reached out to a community wider than its undergraduates, not least as a public relations exercise to make the College better known. There were study days organised for teachers, for example, to up-date them on more recent thinking in scripture or on theological topics. There were evening courses, sometimes Heythrop's own, sometimes run under the aegis of the Extra-Mural Department of Birkbeck College - a very successful instance of the latter was a course on feminist religious thought, one of the earliest of its kind in the country, taught by two Heythrop graduates. But useful though they were in raising the profile of the College, they did little for its finances. And there was the added problem that it was sometimes difficult to persuade some members of staff to take part - they had, they argued, their own networks which they served. The Masters degrees, on the other hand, were not only profitable to the College, for the most part they were taught during the day and were clearly part of Heythrop's programme, thus drawing upon staff from all of the teaching departments.

There was a further initiative to raise awareness of the College: the publication between 1976 and 1990 of a series of 'Heythrop Monographs'

1 The Bishop of London, the Right Reverend Richard Chartres, made a point of thanking Heythrop in the person of the present writer on an occasion when they were introduced for the service that its programmes were providing for the clergy of his Church of England diocese.

inspired originally by the desire of a couple of members of staff to have their theses published, the first scriptural, the second patristic. The Monographs achieved a modest success, particularly that by Gerard J. Hughes on *Authority in Morals*, and were eventually taken under the wing of the Catholic publishing company Sheed and Ward. Only seven were produced, though there should have been more: a series that had been commissioned on the theology of Karl Rahner by the Hungarian Jesuit George Vass, who had long been teaching at Heythrop but later went to a professorship in the theology faculty in Innsbruck, Austria, just bore the Sheed and Ward imprint. *The Heythrop Journal* continued to be edited from Cavendish Square, with a wider range of contributors. And members of staff occasionally published books and articles. The publications of one member of the Philosophy Department, however, deserve special mention. A former accountant, Peter Vardy, became a member of the Philosophy Department after his doctorate at King's College. In 1990 he published *The Puzzle of God*, to be followed by a series of further "Puzzle" books: *of Evil* (1992), *of the Gospels* (1995), *of Sex* (1997), *of Ethics* (1999). They led to invitations to speak in schools, at sixth-form conferences, at prize days and so on, and he proved to have a remarkable ability to communicate with young people. This led to a flow of recruits from schools into Heythrop, of which he became Vice Principal from 1999 to 2011. This happened, however, after the College had left its first London home in Cavendish Square for a new site in Kensington Square.

HEYTHROP COLLEGE, LONDON W8, 1993

Although there had been financial considerations, the College's move from the country to central London was largely for ideological reasons, the desire to be in an urban setting and to be associated with a major British university. The move from Central to West London, however, was dictated solely by finance. The owners of the Cavendish Square site, the Sisters of the Holy Child Jesus, needed to provide for their elderly members and were obliged to either sell the property, or to raise the rent Heythrop was paying to a level which the College would have found simply unsupportable. Hence the decision was taken to relocate to another former graduate training college, Maria Assumpta, beside the underground railway line in Kensington Square, a college owned by the Religious of the Assumption.

They had been there since long before the railway line came into existence: the tracks were laid on their dairy farm. They ran a school for the children of the poor, which over the years was transformed into an establishment for teaching children using the Montessori method of education, and a teacher training college. As a training college Maria Assumpta had closed in July 1978, much to the indignation of London's local paper, the *Evening Standard*, which reported that in the course of the previous fifteen years the government had spent some £100,000 building a hostel for 150 students, a state-of-the-art gymnasium and a small language laboratory.[1] That the College was to close had been known for some time, and much thought had been given to the future of the property. A number of agencies moved in - the (Anglican) National Society for Religious Education, the (Catholic) Westminster Religious Education Centre and the Westminster Adult Religious Education Centre, as well as the Westminster Pastoral Foundation (a psychotherapy training unit with various offshoots which, despite its name, had nothing to do with the previous two, or indeed with the Catholic Church at all, at least directly) and the Dyslexia Teaching Centre. There was also, and rather obviously, LAMDA, the London Academy of Music and the Dramatic Arts - "rather obviously" because from the windows of the refectory diners could watch budding actors practising sword fights on the lawn outside. Even after the demise of the training college the hostel continued to be run as a

1 Issue of 18 November 1976.

residence for young women.[1]

Back in the mid-1970s Johnny Maher, once again Principal, albeit briefly, after Copleston's retirement, expressed considerable interest in Maria Assumpta as an alternative to Cavendish Square. He took several members of staff, individually, on exploratory visits. He reported that, given the annual intake of Heythrop at the time, the Kensington Square site would prove to be too big, though it could be shared with other educational agencies such as those just mentioned. The student hostel, he thought, might be both a blessing and a curse - though he chose to describe it as an albatross. Even two decades or so earlier, therefore, the possibility of Kensington Square had been actively considered. As Maher wrote in a letter to Mahoney, "The space at Cavendish Square is very limited and seems to me to place narrow limits on future developments".[2] In the end it was rejected on financial grounds: the cost of renting sufficient space, it was calculated, would have been at the time 50% more than the College was paying at Cavendish Square.

When the move from Cavendish Square was again raised in the light of the proposed change in the rental agreement there was much opposition from faculty members. There were many reasons. Kensington was not as easy to reach as Cavendish Square: it might have been just about as close to an underground station, but Oxford Circus was well served, whilst High Street Kensington was not. It was, moreover, much further away from the University's Senate House, to which staff had to go for meetings and staff and students to borrow books from the Senate House Library. This was a far less significant factor in the early 1990s than it would have been in the mid-1970s. When Heythrop came to London the University operated much more as a federal institution than it has done since the mid-1990s. Degrees were frequently taught federally - Philosophy being one of the last to become entirely college-based. Even the (practically) University-wide Library computer system collapsed into component parts, though Heythrop remained closely tied to Senate House Library. Closeness to the central University complex in Bloomsbury was therefore of much less importance than

1 This paragraph relies on the opening address for the Academic Year 1993-94 by Brendan Callaghan, the Principal at the time of the move, a shortened version of which was published in LLNN 92 (Summer 1994), pp. 5-9.

2 Letter dated 5 August 1976 in Heythrop Archive file headed "Fr Maher's correspondence".

it had been. But staff members were comfortable in Cavendish Square, and some argued fiercely that the English Jesuits ought either to find the increased rental or to buy the site outright which, wisely, the Jesuits refused to do.[1]

The move to Kensington Square was not a foregone conclusion. There were members of the governing body who argued for an amalgamation of Heythrop with some other London college, and relocation to its campus. Mergers were very much in the air at the time: Bedford College had largely merged with Royal Holloway out at Egham, though some faculties went elsewhere, and Westfield College had been absorbed by Queen Mary College in London's East End. There was also another problem with the proposed new site for the College: Maria Assumpta did not have large enough library accommodation to house Heythrop's collection. This problem was never wholly solved, and a fairly large proportion of Heythrop's holdings had to be housed off-site, at the University's depositary out at Egham. In the end a new library had to be created by adapting the gymnasium: the inside was stripped out, moveable stacks installed on the ground floor and a reading room with more stacks built as a mezzanine. This contained the Theology library while Philosophy books, and periodicals, were located in the original, and rather elegant, Maria Assumpta library. There was also a large reference room collection.

There were some very real benefits of moving to West London which, thanks to steady improvements in the underground rail system, proved eventually not to be quite so difficult to reach as many had feared. There was catering available to the students, a facility which had early been abandoned at Cavendish Square on grounds of cost. In Kensington it had to be maintained for the residents in the hostel but was therefore also available to all who wished to use it. There was a pleasant garden. There was much more lecture room space, including a large hall for major events. As one member of staff, Michael Kirwan, commented, echoing what Maher had written twenty years earlier, "As it turned out, we would have been 'trapped' in the site had we stayed [in Cavendish Square], because we could not have expanded as we did in Kensington".[2]

And expand the College certainly did. At the time of the move the

1 The Cavendish Square property was eventually sold to the King's Fund, an independent health service think-tank.

2 Michael Kirwan, "Heythrop College in 2009" in LLNN 2009, p. 111.

number of students, undergraduate and postgraduate, was not yet 300. By the time Dr Kirwan was writing in 2009 the total number was almost 1,000. They were coming to a somewhat different environment than had the first group to arrive in Kensington Square. After long and complex negotiations the British Province of the Society of Jesus had purchased the Maria Assumpta campus in February 2009 - apparently the most costly single acquisition of real estate that the Province had ever launched upon - and leased it to the College at a peppercorn rent for a period of 70 years. The purchase almost used up the money the Jesuits had made available to support the College in what was called the Bellarmine Fund. It was no longer available to subsidise Heythrop, but on the other hand Heythrop was now able to rent out for its own benefit parts of the property to other appropriate organisations - the major one being the Jesuit-run Fordham University of New York. Ownership of the property by the Jesuits also meant that the College could engage on major improvements to the site for the benefit of students and staff, though particularly the former. In another major change the faculty also decided to abandon the practice, adopted at the very beginning of its time in London, of treating every one of its members as of equal standing, and gradually introduced the titles of Senior Lecturer and Professor. This was all part of the process of "normalisation", making the College more like other equivalent institutions in the country.

Whatever individual members of staff may have thought of "normalisation", both the word and the process was wished upon the College by Whitehall. It will be remembered that when Heythrop entered the University of London in 1970 it did so as a non-grant-receiving institution. That meant that while the College itself did not receive money directly from the State the students did so, and to compensate the College somewhat for a lack of a grant students at Heythrop received rather more money to pay their fees than did those studying at King's or other colleges. One aspect of universities' accountability to government and public are periodic visits from the Quality Assurance Agency. The first such visit to Heythrop was made in 2001; others occurred in 2005 and 2011. The QAA looks at the quality and standards of teaching and their visits served a useful purpose in bringing Heythrop's systems into line with the mainstream of higher education institutions. Despite the punishing exercise, the results were a strong endorsement of the College's teaching.

Heythrop's integration into the Research Assessment Exercise (the RAE), now known as the "Research Excellence Framework" (REF), has taken rather longer. Money for research did not come to the College from the Higher Education Funding Council (HEFCE, the successor to the University Grants Committee) until 2006, and the RAE took place in 2008 so the College had little time to prepare. Nonetheless the results were perceived by some as disappointing, certainly as compared to other institutions within the field of theology and religious studies, including the Catholic foundations, as was pointed out in an article which appeared in *The Tablet*, the Catholic weekly. The then Principal, Dr John McDade, came to the College's defence in a letter to the paper, on 10th January 2009: "About half the outputs were found to be of an international quality with a large proportion at a quality recognised nationally," he wrote.[1] In an interview published a month later, while Peter Vardy acknowledged that the College needed to do better, he also pointed to 'ground-breaking' academic courses and added "We have three of probably the best-known people in schools in terms of philosophy of religion and ethics, and, six years ago, we were the first in the country to introduce a degree in philosophy, religion and ethics". The article went on:

> The mission to reach out to others also includes extensive work in interreligious dialogue, and a BA in Abrahamic Faiths, the first of its kind in Europe, was launched two years ago. This has led to a rather impressive example of Islamic-Jewish friendship. "Last year [Vardy was quoted as saying] we had an Orthodox Jew, Jonathan Gorsky, sharing an office with Mohammad Shomali, a professor from Qom in Iran, the biggest centre of theological formation in Shia Islam".[2]

Nonetheless it was true that, over many years, research had not been as high a priority for the College[3] as teaching: in a survey of student satisfaction with teaching and learning in all comparable UK institutions, Heythrop's teaching was marked at 92%, well above the national average. In the same article in

1 *The Tablet*, 10 January 2009, p. 21.

2 *The Tablet*, 7 February 2009, p. 48.

3 The present writer had commented on this missing dimension of the college two decades earlier. See Michael Walsh, "Jesuits in the University", *The Tablet* 19th February 1983, pp. 18-19.

The Tablet in January 2009, Peter Vardy acknowledged that the College needed to develop its research profile. This it set about doing. A director of research and research fellows were appointed. New centres and institutes were founded to develop the research environment of the College: the Religious Life Institute, the Centre for Eastern Christianity, the Centre for Christianity and Interreligious Dialogue, the Centre for Philosophy of Religion and the Heythrop Institute: Religion and Society.

Heythrop had been happy to enter the HEFCE funding system as in the first instance it meant receiving more money. Moreover, as members of staff occasionally realised, being outside the general structure of university funding led to a number of entirely non-financial complications. But being part of HEFCE also meant greater accountability and thus much greater need for administration. This was fine in itself, but student numbers had to grow quickly to pay for the new members of administrative staff. Entry into HEFCE also coincided with fundamental changes to nation-wide university funding; from 2012 the money followed the student rather than there being a grant to an institution. At the same time controls on how many new undergraduates a college might take were being gradually removed.

The impact of these changes cannot be foreseen and in any case lies outside an account of its history,[1] but the College is taking steps to minimise any potential damage. One important recent innovation is the link with the Catholic University of Louvain (Leuven). When the College moved to Liège, as has been remarked,[2] the University of Louvain stood in the way of the English College, or its Walloon counterpart, becoming a university in its own right. Now it is collaborating with Heythrop to allow those who need them to acquire an ecclesiastical degree in theology. This development occasioned some comment outside the College on the grounds that "seminary" qualifications were not regarded as academically rigorous as the degrees of British universities.

1 There is a highly critical article on current policy in higher education by Stefan Collini in *The London Review of Books*, Vol. 35 No. 20 (24 October 2013), pp. 3-12 which shows how it will impact on, especially, the study of the Humanities. Collini is Professor of English at Cambridge, and his article - strictly speaking a very long book review - is entitled "Sold Out".

2 See above, p. 12.

Such criticism was, and is, is misplaced. Those, predominantly clerical, students who require such ecclesiastical qualifications for their future careers will first have to pass their London degrees as well as their Church-related ones. Just such a plan was in the minds of those who, in 1969-1970, were negotiating for the College to join the University of London. At the time it was not acceptable: now it is.

The College has gone further. In November 1964 Rome granted Heythrop the right to award ecclesiastical degrees, the "Licences" in Theology (S.T.L.) and in Philosophy (Lic. Phil.) to non-Jesuits. As has been seen, these fell into abeyance after the College moved to London, but were reactivated on 17th September 2013, the feast of St Robert Bellarmine, the College's patron saint, by the Congregation for Catholic Education. Teaching specific to these degrees is now located in the Bellarmine Institute which, as the website says, exists:

- to serve the Church and the common good by providing a full range of programmes in the first, second and third cycles leading to the award of baccalaureate, licentiate and doctorate degrees;
- to collaborate closely in the work of evangelization with the Hierarchy and with the local and the universal Church and
- to establish fruitful collaboration with other ecclesiastical faculties and with non-ecclesiastical faculties and centres of Theology and Philosophy.

All these programmes are taught in conjunction with the equivalent degree of the University of London. Such a development was perhaps inevitable after Heythrop had been designated by the Jesuit headquarters in Rome as "an official centre of [Jesuit] formation in Europe, as part of the plan to rationalise the number of such centres by about two-thirds".[1]

As it begins its fifth century of existence, the College which is now Heythrop still has, unlike many other such foundations, even John Carroll's mighty Georgetown, a Jesuit at its helm. But it also has, overseeing its academic progress, a vice-principal who undertook undergraduate and doctoral studies

1 Kirwan, "Heythrop College in 2009" p. 113.

at Heythrop before moving on and becoming a professor at another College of the University of London. It is almost as if the Jesuit tradition of a teaching institution being governed by a rector with a prefect of studies in charge of the curriculum had been revived in a rather more contemporary form. There is, however, one big difference from the traditional practice: in this instance the "Prefect of Studies" role is performed by a woman, Gwen Griffith-Dickson.

The first women to penetrate what had been, for three and a half centuries, an exclusively male domain were four feisty nuns who arrived in 1965 at the launch of the Pontifical Athenaeum. In 1970, as the College opened in Cavendish Square, there were five religious sisters and four laywomen, just nine women in all out of a total enrolment in that first year of 112. The proportion of women increased after the move to London, but one convent-school educated alumna remarked on her astonishment at the dominance of deep male voices as hymns were sung at the mass for the opening of the 1971-72 academic year. The number of women studying for a degree in theology soon came to rival that of male students. In those early years Heythrop was the only place in the British Isles where women could study alongside men for a university degree in Catholic theology. "It was very empowering", recalled another alumna who went on, like other of her female contemporaries, to a distinguished academic career in religious studies: "The staff took us seriously as theologians".[1]

So to return to the question of continuity raised at the beginning of this history, would those Jesuit scholastics who first gathered at St John's in Louvain find anything familiar in Heythrop College, University of London? They would undoubtedly be startled by the presence of women in the student body, but other things would be familiar. Even some of the theology they might well recognise, though probably less of the philosophy. They were exiles in Louvain, fleeing the persecution of their faith and aware that there was a very real chance that some of their number might be martyred. Some Heythrop

1 The comments of the two alumnae were in private conversations while preparing this book. After the Society of Jesus decided that Heythrop is to be its only English-speaking theologate in Europe, the balance of men against women is again shifting in favour of the former, as Jesuit scholastics arrive from many different parts of the world.

students, even since the move to London, have been killed in a manner reminiscent of martyrdom, though no one is claiming that title for them. The Louvain scholastics, and even those in the first century or so at Liège, would be astonished to learn that the institution that prepared them for the priesthood now operates in Britain under a royal charter, and with a grant of arms, but if they poked about for long enough in the Library they might still come across books which their professors had instructed them to read, not least a shelf-full of Robert Bellarmine's *De Controversiis*. They would not, however, find controversy, or polemics, on the curriculum but instead a theology which is ecumenical, and an intense study of the beliefs and practices of other world religions.

When in the autumn of 1926 the Jesuit scholastics from St Mary's Hall and those from St Beuno's College gathered for the first time to begin their studies at Heythrop in Oxfordshire, a third of their number belonged to Provinces of the Society other than that of England. That is something which the students at Louvain or Liège would not have been expecting. But it is now something which Heythrop expects and takes in its stride. As Brendan Callaghan remarked in his address to mark the first year at Kensington Square, the College has brought together:

> into one collegiate community a range of backgrounds only partially illustrated by labels of nationality or creed. The person next to whom you are sitting may come from any one of thirty countries, covering four of the five continents, from one of many Christian denominations, from another faith-tradition entirely, or from a non-religious background. They may be a school-leaver or a grand-parent, on their way to ordination or hoping to spend their life in academic work, beginning their studies, resuming an interrupted education, or enjoying a sabbatical. They may be an ordained minister, or a religious brother or sister; they may share your outlook on life almost entirely, or be about to surprise you with the different viewpoint they offer. But what is important is that for this next year, or two years, or three years, you and they are equally part of this academic community called Heythrop.[1]

1 Brendan Callaghan, "Heythrop College, Kensington Square" in LLNN 92 (Summer 1994), p. 7.

SELECT BIBLIOGRAPHY

Brinkman, Bruno SJ, "The making of the Heythrop Athenaeum" in *Letters and Notices* 89 (1989)

Butterworth, Robert, *The Detour: Towards Revising Catholicism* (Leominster: Gracewing, 2005)

Callaghan, Brendan SJ, "Heythrop College, Kensington Square" in *Letters and Notices* 92 (1994)

Caraman, Philip SJ, *The University of the Nations* (New York, Paulist Press, 1981)

Caruana, Louis SJ, "The Jesuits and the scientific revolution" in Thomas Worcester (ed.), *The Cambridge Companion to the Jesuits* (Cambridge University Press, 2008)

Chadwick, Hubert SJ, St *Omers to Stonyhurst* (London, Burns and Oates, 1962)

Champ, Judith F., "Milner, John (1752-1826)", *Oxford Dictionary of National Biography* (Oxford University Press, 2004);

Copleston, Frederick C. SJ, *Memoirs of a Philosopher* (Kansas City MO, Sheed and Ward, 1993)

Edwards, Francis SJ, *The Jesuits in England* (Tunbridge Wells, Burns and Oates, 1985)

Edwards, Paul SJ, *Canutes's Tower* (Leominster, Gracewing, 1990)

Foley, Henry SJ, *Records of the English Province of the Society of Jesus*, vol. V (London, Burns and Oates, 1879)

Guérin, Pierre SJ, "Le coutumier des Jésuites anglais de Liège (1633) *Bulletin de l'Institut archeologique Liègeois* t. C. (1988)

Hanley, Thomas O'Brien SJ (ed.), *The John Carroll Papers* (Notre Dame: University of Notre Dame Press, c. 1976), 3 vols.

Gillow, Joseph, *Bibliographical Dictionary of the English Catholics* (London, Burns and Oates, 1885- 1902, five vols.)

Guilday, Peter, *The Life and Times of John Carroll* (New York, The Encyclopedia Press, 1922).

Holmes, Peter (ed.), *Caroline Casuistry: The Cases of Conscience of Fr Thomas Southwell SJ* (Woodbridge, The Boydell Press for the Catholic Record Society, 2012)

Holt, Geoffrey SJ, "The English Jesuits at Liège and Chevremont" in *Chevremont Un tricentaire, Un millenaire* (1988)

Holt, Geoffrey SJ, *William Strickland and the Restored Jesuits* (London, Society of Jesus, 1988)

Kirwan, Michael SJ, "Heythrop College in 2009" in *Letters and Notices* 99

Mahoney, John SJ, "Heythrop's Move to London, 1970. A Personal Reminiscence" Part I, *Letters and Notices* 99 (2009)

Mahoney, John SJ, "Heythrop's Move to London, 1970. A Personal Reminiscence" Part II, *Letters and Notices* 99 (2010)

Marković, Zeljko, "Boscovich's *Theoria*" in Lancelot Law (ed.), *Roger Joseph Boscovich* (London, Allen and Unwin, 1961)

Matthew, David, *Catholicism in England, 1535-1935* (London, Longmans, 1936)

McClelland, Vincent Allen, *English Roman Catholics and Higher Education, 1830-1903* (Oxford, Clarendon Press, 1973)

McCoog, Thomas M. SJ, *The Society of Jesus in England 1623-1688: An Institutional Study* (unpublished doctoral dissertation, Warwick University, May 1984)

McCoog, Thomas M. SJ, (ed.), *Promising Hope* (Rome, Institutum Historicum Societatis Iesu, 2003)

Melville, Annabelle, *John Carroll of Baltimore* (New York: Charles Scribner, 1955)

Milward, Peter SJ, *Religious Controversies of the Jacobean Age: A Survey of Printed Sources* (London, Scolar Press, 1978)

Newman, John Henry, *Historical Sketches*, Vol. 2, (London, Longmans Green & Co., 1899)

Oliver, George, *Collections towards illustrating the Biography of the Scotch, English and Irish Members S.J.* (Exeter, W. C. Featherstone, 1838)

O'Malley, John W. SJ, *The First Jesuits* (Cambridge MA, Harvard University Press, 1993)

O'Malley, John W. SJ *et al.*, (eds.), *The Jesuits II: Cultures, Sciences and the Arts, 154-1773* (University of Toronto Press, 2006)

Opsomer, Camélia, "Un foyer d'études sous l'Ancien Régime: le Collège des Jésuites anglais de Liège" *Bulletin de l'Académie Royale de Belgique*, 6e série, t. XII, 1-6 (2001), pp. 11-39, but see http://www.gedhs.ulg.ac.be/ebibliotheque/articles/opsomer/college.html#asterisque.

Petre, M. D. (ed.), *Autobiography of George Tyrrell* (London, Edward Arnold, 1912)

Pollen, John Hungerford SJ, *The Life and Letters of Father John Morris SJ* (London, Burns and Oates, 1896)

Redworth, Glyn, *The She-Apostle: The Extraordinary Life and Death of Luisa de Carvajal* (Oxford University Press, 2008).

Reilly, Conor SJ, *Francis Line S.J. An Exiled English Scientist, 1595-1675* (Rome: Institutum Historicum Societatis Iesu, 1969)
Rhodes, Elizabeth, "Join the Jesuits, See the World: Early Modern Women" in John W. O'Malley *et al.*, (eds.), *The Jesuits II: Cultures, Sciences and the Arts, 154-1773* (University of Toronto Press, 2006)
Schultenover, David SJ, *George Tyrrell: In Search of Catholicism* (Shepherdstown, The Patmos Press, 1981)
Schultenover, David SJ, *A View From Rome* (New York, Fordham University Press, 1993)
Sire, H.J.A, *Gentlemen Philosophers* (Worthing, Churchman Publishing, 1988)
Sutcliffe, Edmund SJ, *Bibliography of the English Province of the Society of Jesus, 1773-1953* (London, Manresa Press, 1957)
This Tight Embrace: Luisa de Carvajal y Mendoza (1566-1614), edited, translated and introduced by Elizabeth Rhodes (Milwaukee, Marquette University Press, 2000)
Thomas, Alfred SJ, *Hopkins the Jesuit: The years of training* (London, Oxford University Press, 1969)
Walsh, Michael, "Jesuits in the university", *The Tablet* 19th February 1983, pp. 18-19
Walsh, Michael, *The Cardinals* (Norwich, The Canterbury Press, 2010)
Whitehead, Maurice, "In the Sincerest Intentions of Studying": The Educational Legacy of Thomas Weld (1750-1810)", *Recusant History* 26 (2002-2003), pp. 169-193
Whitehead, Maurice, "A prolific nursery of piety and learning", in Thomas M.McCoog (ed.), *Promising Hope* (Rome, Institutum Historicum Societatis Iesu, 2003)
Whitehead, Maurice, "Education and Correct Conduct": Randal Lythgoe and the work of the Society of Jesus in early Victorian England and Wales" in Sheridan Gilley (ed.), *Victorian Churches and Churchmen: Essays Presented to Vincent Alan McClelland* (Woodbridge, The Boydell Press for the Catholic Record Society, 2005)
Whitehead, Maurice, *English Jesuit Education: Expulsion, Suppression, Survival and Restoration, 1762-1803* (Farnham, Ashgate, 2013)
Whyte, Lancelot Law (ed.), *Roger Joseph Boscovich* (London, Allen and Unwin, 1961)
Worcester, Thomas SJ (ed.), *The Cambridge Companion to the Jesuits* (Cambridge University Press, 2008)

INDEX OF PERSONS

INDEX OF PERSONS

INDEX OF PERSONS

INDEX OF PERSONS